Marketing Made for Celebrants

Boost Your Bookings With Easy and Effective Marketing Methods

Marketing Made Easy for Celebrants
Boost Your Bookings With Easy and Effective Marketing Methods

Anita Revel

ISBN 978-0-9804439-6-7

Published by   Now Age Publishing Pty Ltd
                      PO Box 555, Cowaramup 6284
                      Western Australia
                      NowAgePublishing.com

Cover by   Inspired Insight
                      inspired-insight.com

National Library of Australia Cataloguing-in-Publication entry

Author: Revel, Anita, 1968-

Title: Marketing made easy for civil celebrants : boost your
                      bookings with easy and effective marketing
                      methods / by Anita Revel.

ISBN: 9780980443967 (pbk.)

Subjects: Marriage celebrants--Australia.
                      Rites and ceremonies--Australia.
                      Small business marketing--Australia.
                      Small business--Management--Australia.

Dewey Number: 338.761

Marketing Made Easy for Celebrants

Boost Your Bookings With Easy and Effective Marketing Methods

ANITA REVEL

now age
PUBLISHING

With Gratitude

With thanks to Australian Civil Celebrants and wedding industry professionals who contributed to this edition...
Charles Foley, Bilawara Lee, Kathy Speake, Robert Simmons, Maggie Magee, David Read, Lyn Fox and Dally Messenger III.

Thanks also to my northern hemisphere colleagues, Heather Martin, Jill Z McBride, Thomas Witham, Kenneth 'Cat Daddy' Pogson, Tres Shannon, Vivi O'Stara and Jay Moore.

Table of Contents

Foreword by Charles Foley CMC

Today I asked an Aboriginal friend and elder: "How long have indigenous people been commemorating life events? Was it, as some say, 40,000 or 60,000 or 80,000 years? Her answer was simple and wise: "Since the beginning!"

We know that ceremony is our human way of observing significant shifts in life's flow. We know that she, you and I are one of 35,000 or more registered Celebrants appointed by the government to officiate at weddings. We know that there are numerous appointed and non-appointed Civil Celebrants who conduct child, boat, truck namings; human and pet funerals and memorials; home/apartment-flat/house warmings and blessings; gay/lesbian/bi/transgender and de facto civil partnerships/unions/commitments; renewal of vows and reaffirmations of commitment; solstice and seasonal celebrations; retirement and other work related or corporate events; generic civic and personalised family citizenship ceremonies; reconciliation events; divorce/separation/blending-family presentations; organ donation ceremonies; anniversary/birthday celebrations; coming of age/menarche celebrations; and so much more. But what we don't always know is the best way to *market* all of our services.

Here is a book from a most knowledgeable marketing expert who is also a recently appointed Civil Celebrant. Anita has done her research within the craft of celebrancy and has endeavoured to place the rest of us within our special place within the wedding industry, and within the ranks of other performance artists within civil celebrancy. I've already begun incorporating her ideas into my own marketing strategy!

Anita has written "… times change…" and so they have.
I started as an Officiant in the USA in 1971, and as a Civil
Celebrant in Australia in 1991. Back then there was no
Generation X or Generation Y. In fact, until I read this book
I had only an inaccurate and incomplete idea about how to
market myself to my contemporary Baby Boomers, and
absolutely no thoughts about the coming Generation Z!

If you are a hobbyist Celebrant, or if you are a philanthropist
who likes funding the celebrations of others, or if you are in
the celebrancy craft for the pure fun of it or for the applause of
being a performance artist, then this book may not be for you.

But if you like the idea of working smarter not harder; if you
want to earn some monetary rewards for your efforts, then
pay attention to this easy to read text that is 'chocka block' full
of practical tips, suggestions and thoughtful strategies.

When I sold my own book, *Your Guide to Becoming a Successful
Civil Celebrant*, in the mid 1990s, I guaranteed that if the
aspiring Civil Celebrant didn't make the $65 cost of the book
back at the first ceremony, after following my directions, then
I would refund the full price upon return of the book. No one
returned the book! I can tell you that by using Anita's
suggestions you too will continuously reap the benefits for
years to come, just as surely.

And a parting hint: photocopy the worksheets and fill them
out anew every few months. Times change; so do the effects
of your marketing.

Charles R Foley

'Charles the Celebrant' :: www.celebrantservices.com.au

Objectives of This Handbook

I became an authorised Civil Marriage Celebrant in 2008, right alongside hundreds of other new Celebrants simultaneously registered by the Attorney General.

At first I was intimidated by the prospect of building my celebrancy business with such an influx of competition all at once. Where there were just under 3,500 Commonwealth registered marriage celebrants in 2003, this figure jumped to over 10,000 by April 2010. This doesn't include the 23,700 or so ministers of religion, registered by State and Territory registering authorities to solemnise marriages[1].

Having completed my training by correspondence years earlier, I was the greenest-of-green Celebrants being unleashed right in the middle of the tidal wave of new registrations. Added to this, the lead-time for building a solid celebrancy business takes years of hard work!

Starting the process was a frightening prospect. I soon realised my fears were unfounded, however, when I began networking with other Celebrants and discovered:

a)   Many new Celebrants had been on the registration waiting list so long they'd gone rusty since their training and were tentative about starting their celebrancy business;

b)   Others didn't have the first clue about how to get their name 'out there' – they paid for a link on a website here and there and that was it for their marketing efforts;

---

[1] http://www.ag.gov.au/celebrants

c) Judging by comments in the Celebrant forums, most Celebrants were in need of quality marketing advice; and

d) Within hours of having my email address published on the Attorney General's website, I began receiving dozens of unsolicited emails from other Celebrants and industry professionals offering their software, design packages, web-page design services, training programs, advertising subscriptions and so on... Most alarmingly, every single email I received was sent illegally. *Every. Single. One.* I was shocked that these business owners, though proficient in their own fields, weren't up to speed on the legalities and ethics of running a marketing campaign.

For all the reasons listed above, I decided to do something about sharing what I know about marketing with my fellow Celebrants.

My marketing experience comes mainly from agency-side work for large corporates and government agencies, but the principles of marketing remain true for all business models and sizes. I'll be outlining these principles in this book, as well as providing worksheets and step-by-step prompts to encourage you to create your own marketing strategies easily, cost-effectively and ethically.

It should be noted, however, that while this guide is full of real-life examples and case studies, the ideas offered are intended to trigger *original* ideas within you. Copying the ideas directly may not work for you and your particular situation. If you're ever in doubt, contact a reputable marketing agency or consultant to help you out.

In the meantime, put on your creative thinking cap, and let's go!

Why You Need a Marketing Strategy

> "Some regard private enterprise as if it were a predatory tiger to be shot. Others look upon it as a cow that they can milk. Only a handful see it for what it really is – the strong horse that pulls the whole cart."
>
> ~ Winston Churchill

There are two types of Civil Celebrants... the first is the Civil Marriage Celebrant appointed by the Attorney General. This Celebrant must trade in his or her name and not as a registered business. The second type of Civil Celebrant offers a range of services such as funeral officiancy or baby-naming ceremonies, and may trade under a business name.

There is a third type of Celebrant, also registered to conduct weddings by the Attorney General, but which is not classed as Civil – this is the ordained minister, priest or other Officiant conducting weddings on behalf of their religious institution.

For the sake of convenience, all three situations are referred to in this book as 'celebrancy' throughout. We are all united by a common love of ceremony and celebration after all.

Whether you're promoting your celebrancy services in your own name, under the name of business, or even as an Officiant via your church or other religious institution, a good marketing plan is your key to getting the most bookings for the smallest marketing budget possible.

The advice in this book is designed to show you ways to create and implement your own marketing strategies at low cost and low risk, which will grow your business for no effort once you've set it up.

In fact, by the end of it you will be able to:

1. Demonstrate an understanding of what marketing is;

2. Know which types of marketing activities to engage in;

3. Build a sticky brand and branding elements;

4. Save money on your advertising spend in line with your Five Ps of marketing;

5. Incorporate a call-to-action in every campaign you do;

6. Sky-rocket your bookings with your uniqueness;

7. Optimise your marketing spend by tracking your ROI;

8. Boost your search engine rankings; and

9. Evaluate the success of your marketing campaign in terms of spend and results.

There are a series of worksheets and homework suggestions included in Chapter 13. I encourage you to use them as you work your way through this book.

If you shudder at the thought of jotting notes in books, well, I don't care if you photocopy the worksheets for personal use[2]; I only care that you use them!

---

[2] Refer to the section on the Copyright Act 1968 in Chapter 12 for further information on 'personal use'.

What is Marketing?

Marketing can be defined as your business' strategy for satisfying the needs, wants and demands of consumers. When done effectively, it alleviates the need for a sales pitch or effort – in other words, your product or service will sell itself.

Marketing affects nearly every aspect of your business, from how you'll spend your advertising budget, to how much you will charge for your services. It also helps you set yourself apart from the competition and build a healthy reputation in the industry.

Marketing is not one thing a company does to attract potential customers; it is everything a company does.

Marketing incorporates a variety of components, including:

- package design
- branding
- sales
- advertising
- promotion
- e-commerce
- market research
- focus testing and evaluation
- networking
- sponsorship
- customer relations
- public relations

In addition, marketing is:

- **Ongoing**. Most businesses can rely on repeat business to stay profitable. Celebrants, on the other hand, rely on a constant flow of new customers for one-off business transactions. Customers hire us for a wedding service, a funeral service, to name their first-born… all once-in-a-lifetime services (generally!). Therefore, Celebrants need to prioritise *ongoing* marketing practices to attract new business every week.

- **Imperative**. Every business must find customers; most businesses need to retain them. Without a plan, however, businesses will neither find them nor retain them. New business owners should create a plan prior to advertising; those in business for a while should continually update this plan to address changes that occur over time.

- **Ever-changing**. Marketing tactics are constantly emerging and evolving in response to technology and shifts in consumer behaviour. Virtual marketing, for example, has really gained momentum in the last ten years. Dot com companies such as Facebook, which reaches nearly 175 million people every day, has opened even newer doors for businesses hoping to reach a vast amount of potential customers. As times change, so do marketing techniques; smart business owners will keep up with them.

- **Individualised**. As a Celebrant, your needs are different from that of a car dealer or multi-national. You must determine who you are and what makes you unique to stand out among others in your field. Then use this knowledge to create an individualised marketing plan.

And What it Isn't!

Marketing is not:

- **Ad hoc**, or something you do only if you have the time. You've made the decision to become a Celebrant. You've taken the time to develop your business idea. Now you must allocate some time to a marketing plan, which is a critical component of every successful business.

- **Always Costly**. It can be expensive when you purchase whizz-bang advertising options, but you can also market yourself on a small budget by being creative. In fact, in Chapter 9 I give you 10 ideas for totally free promotion.

- **A one-time shot**. As stated above, marketing is an ongoing process. Campaigns should be evaluated on a regular basis and changed as needed. For example, attending networking events in your hometown might, for a while, produce a large amount of work as you meet new people who know people that need a Celebrant. After attending these events for a while, you might find you've met everyone and the number of new clients you obtain through this outlet slows. This doesn't mean you should give up attending networking events; it means it is time to incorporate other marketing avenues into your campaign to attract a wider clientele.

- **Set-and-forget**, or simply placing a repeat ad in the newspaper. Advertising is one component of a successful campaign, but it is not the only component. Creating a brand, individualising your services, evaluating your marketing efforts, and continually looking at how you might attract new clients is also important.

Legal and Cultural Considerations

There are many forces that affect the marketing environment including competition, laws and regulations, the socio-economic climate in your area, and cultural factors.

Competition

There are no prescribed fees set by the Commonwealth for Civil Celebrants – instead, we have the freedom to charge a fee we consider appropriate to recover our costs and make a living. When setting your fees ensure they are fair, represent value for money, and are independently set despite what the competition is charging.

Laws and Regulations

All individuals and businesses are required to observe their obligations under the law, whether that be under the Trade Practices Act or the Competition Code. Celebrants in particular have a Code of Practice they must comply with, which states, in part:

A marriage celebrant must:

(a) solemnise marriages according to the legal requirements of the Marriage Act 1961 (Cth); and

(b) observe the laws of the Commonwealth and of the State or Territory where the marriage is to be solemnised; and

(c) prevent and avoid unlawful discrimination in the provision of marriage celebrancy services.

There are other Acts that you need to comply with when marketing your services, and they are the Privacy Act (if you're collecting personal details) and the Spam Act (if you're marketing via the internet). These are examined further in Chapter 11.

Socio-Economic Climate

The area in which you operate affects the type of product you offer and the value you place on that product. Celebrants in popular tourist destinations will have a different price-point and level of service than those living in lower-density regions of Australia. Make sure your service and fees are appropriate to your area and target audience.

Cultural Factors

Australia has a rich culture made up a multitude of sub-cultures that include nationality, religion, generation and geographic regions. When creating your marketing message it's imperative that you understand your target market's culture. What do they consider appropriate behaviour? What can they be offended by that you should avoid? What entices them to act? What are their values?

An emerging trend in Australia is to acknowledge our land's original custodians at the start of every gathering. This is being particularly encouraged by the Australians for Native Title and Reconciliation organisation (ANTaR[3]), and is referred to as Acknowledging Country, or a Welcome to Country if spoken by an indigenous person. As well as speaking it at the start of your ceremonies, ANTaR suggests including an acknowledgment on websites, email signatures, and at the

---

[3] www.antar.org.au

beginning of meetings and events as an ongoing reminder of Aboriginal and Torres Strait Islander survival, custodianship, and struggle.

An example of an Acknowledgement of Aboriginal Custodianship of Country comes from Charles Foley[4], an Officiant from the Canberra region, which he used to open a Coalition of Celebrant Associations (CoCA) meeting in 2009.

"Before we begin the proceedings, I would like to acknowledge and pay respect to the traditional owners of the land upon which we meet – the Cadigal People of the Eora Nation. It is upon their ancestral lands that Humanist House is built. As we share our knowledge, trainings, learnings and opinions within this meeting, may we also pay respect to the knowledge embedded within the Aboriginal Custodianship of Country."

According to Bilawara Lee[5], a Celebrant, Elder and one of the Traditional Custodians from the Larrakia Lands of Darwin, more and more couples are asking for a Welcome to Country to open their weddings. Bilawara uses the following words:

"I wish to acknowledge the Traditional Custodians of the the land we stand on today, and I pay my respects to the Elders past and present."

If you know who the traditional custodians are it's good to mention them, but if you're not sure, Bilawara's version is fine.

The Local Aboriginal Land Councils[6] (LALCs) are very helpful in clarifying as to which group is appropriate for each region. as well as providing pronunciation advice.

---

[4] www.celebrantservices.com.au

[5] www.dirila.com.au

[6] www.alc.org.au

Types of Marketing

"If I had only known, I would have been a locksmith."

~ Albert Einstein

There are hundreds of different and innovative ways to market your services, but none of them will be as effective if you don't do your homework first. That is, work out a strategy on how you're going to get the biggest return on your marketing dollar. Let's start with an overview of all the different types of marketing you could consider.

Traditional Marketing

Also known as **above-the-line marketing**, the seller creates a product, brands the product, then constructs campaigns to convince the customer s/he needs the product. Consumers are often seen as passive participants in the process. Campaigns are generally mainstream, coordinated advertising campaigns designed to instil brand recall into the consumer's brain. In one day the consumer can be exposed to the same brand six times via radio, television, print media, online, direct mail and online. A response from the consumer is rarely required, so the campaigns are difficult to measure for their success rates.

Direct Marketing

Direct marketing suits Small to Medium Enterprises (SME) who don't have the budget to implement a branding campaign. Also known as **below-the-line** marketing, the seller reaches his audience directly using catalogues, direct mail, targeted online ads, telemarketing, expos, fairs and so forth. The communication often addresses the customer directly by name.

The second feature of direct marketing is that it anchors its message with a call-to-action – in order to be considered a successful campaign it is designed to elicit a response from the customer, whether that be a visit to the store or website, a booking, a sale, or simply a phone call for more information. These responses are trackable and measurable thereby enabling the seller to maintain a tight control over the budget and the campaign itself.

Business to Business

Business to business marketing is also referred to as B2B marketing, and as the name suggests, it's the marketing of goods and services to businesses in order to keep them operating. Goods might include equipment, components, raw materials, processing services and supplies, while services could include recruitment, bookkeeping, project management, funeral officiation and travel booking services. The most common B2B markets are manufacturers, resellers, the government and non-profit institutions – businesses that rely on other businesses to survive.

Relationship Marketing

This type of marketing evolved in the 1980s hand in hand with developments in information technology. It is aimed at building and managing trusting and long-term relationships between the seller and the customer. The seller gathers information on its customers, their buying patterns, preferences, feedback and all contact history in a database and uses that information to keep the customer fulfilled, therefore loyal. Because the seller is in constant contact with the customer, campaigns are focused and measurable.

Retail Marketing

When a retailer has foot traffic passing by their front door, they have to act immediately to grab their attention (and their wallet). The messages plastered via signage, window displays, flashing neon lights, spruikers and immediate-delivery mechanisms such as text message and Twitter, all urge the customer to **buy now**!

We've entered a world where Generation Z is already 15 years old (they have never known life without internet), and Generation Alpha is on the horizon. We can shop for anything 24/7; we order books and DVDs on demand. Retailers need to grab our attention and grab it *now*. Everything must go! No payments for six months! Limited time only! Don't miss out! Stocktake sale! Ultimately, the techniques employed create a sense of scarcity and urgency and appeals to the consumer who thrives on immediate gratification.

Viral Marketing

This type of marketing happens just like a virus – it starts with one person spreading the message to 10 people, who in turn share it with 10 more, who in turn share it… until the message has spread to every computer screen (often more than once). The message often comes in the form of an entertaining video or joke, but is only considered marketing if it actually contains a branding strategy or call-to-action that helps your business in a tangible way. Publishing a funny video on YouTube is great if it shows your services in a good light. It's disastrous if it shows you getting the new baby's name wrong or forgetting your lines mid-service.

Multi-Level Marketing (MLM)

Also known as down-the-line marketing, hierarchy marketing, network marketing and person-to-person marketing, MLM is the system by which consumer products are sold directly to consumers. The sales are managed by distributors (usually independent business men and women), and are usually in customers' homes. Think Amway, Nutrimetics, Enjo and other party plan style businesses. The model becomes multi-level when the distributors recruit new distributors and earn a commission from their sales.

Green Marketing

A relatively new style of marketing, this practice takes into consideration consumer concerns about the environment, and actively appeals to their desires to preserve and conserve the planet. 'Green' products – tagged eco-friendly, organic, recyclable, recycled, phosphate-free, carbon offset, refillable, biodegradable, etcetera – have changed the buying habits of consumers and operating practices of businesses all around the world.

Pink Marketing

No, not the art of marketing to women as you might have suspected. The pink market is one of the most lucrative markets in today's economy – it's the gay and lesbian market. Typically, a same-sex couple are DINKies – that is, they enjoy a Double Income No Kids lifestyle, and therefore, in theory have a high disposable income to spend on your products and services. (Bear this in mind when you're deciding on your niche in Chapter 7!)

Types of Marketing a Celebrant Should be Doing

Did you recognise any of your current marketing methods in the descriptions? Who knew marketing is more than sticking an ad in the paper, a line in the Yellow Pages and building a one-page website, right?

Considering most celebrancy businesses are sole operators (and often working from home), Celebrants need to be really smart where they spend their marketing dollar.

Many of the Celebrants I've observed practice above-the-line advertising. They may publish their business card in the paper, in the local business directory, on a couple of major websites and in the portfolios of complementary businesses (such as photographers and reception venues). The branding may be consistent, but the results are hit-and-miss.

This is because very few of them have the one essential element that will prove invaluable to their marketing spend.

It's the element that will take them from the big-budget above-the-line marketing to lower-budget, tightly-monitored below-the-line marketing – the type of marketing most suited to Celebrants. What they're missing is a **call-to-action**.

Call-to-Action

A call-to-action tells your client what you want them to do, as well as how and when. Extended call-to-actions even include why. In short, it's the *what, how, when* and *why* of your ad that will result in bookings.

Broken down, a call-to-action might look like this:

- What you want them to do:
  - Book your services.

- How you want them to do it:
  - By phone
  - Email
  - Fax
  - Web booking form

- When you want them to do it:
  - *Now*!
  - Before (date)

- Why they should do it:
  - Celebrant in high demand – don't miss out!
  - Early-bird booking discount
  - Make the bride's checklist shorter
  - Offer available for a short time only
  - Gift to first six bookings in (month)

A good call-to-action ties in with the goal of your campaign and the tone of your copy – that is, if your goal is to have brides book your services, don't ask them to call you for more information… tell them to *book your services*! Furthermore, ask them to book your services *today*.

Hot words to use in your call-to-action include:

- Book before
- Learn how
- Bonus
- Instant
- Free
- Solve
- Exclusive
- Click here

As well as containing the *what, how, when* and *why* in your call-to-action, an even better call-to-action promotes a sense of scarcity (limited supply!) and urgency (book now!) Here is an example of how Robert Simmons[7], a Celebrant on the Gold Coast, uses call-to-action to boost his bookings.

REDUCED CELEBRANT SERVICE FEES FOR LOCAL WEDDINGS HELD MONDAY TO THURSDAY*

Call now on **0414 913 925** or email to confirm my availability for your special day!

For local Gold Coast Weddings MONDAY TO THURSDAY inclusive

Notice the elements he uses to boost his bookings:

- Call now – the *when*, creates urgency
- Phone and email – the *how*
- Confirm my availability – the *why*, promotes scarcity
- Discount offer – another *why*

Homework: Call-to-Action

Turn to Chapter 13 for a step-by-step worksheet to help you create your own call-to-action.

Once you've decided what your call-to-action is going to be, the next step is working out how you're going to get the word out. This part of the planning stage requires examination and establishment of your Five Ps.

---

[7] www.robertsimmonscelebrant.com.au

The Five Ps / Your Marketing Mix

> "If you don't know where you are going, any road will get you there."
>
> ~ Lewis Carroll

When it comes time to build your marketing plan, getting your marketing mix right will help you get the best return for your promotional dollar. The marketing mix is made up of five variables commonly known as the *Five Ps* of marketing. Vivi O'Stara (Sassy Marketing With Soul[8]) says a basic marketing mix can be created in five minutes providing "…you 'storm' your ideas – you will have plenty of opportunity to finesse them later."

The Five Ps are:

People

The most important 'P' of all is People. Who are they? Where are they? How will they find you? What do they need? What is their motivation for contacting you over any of the other Celebrants they put on their shortlist? How old are they? What are their interests? What do they do in their spare time? Is it the bride that does most of the organising and communication or the groom? And, importantly, what kind of people do you want to attract?

Write down everything you know about clients that contact you, starting with the top three questions they ask you. This

---

[8] www. SassyMarketingWithSoul.com

will give you a starting point to defining their values and priorities. The more you know about your prospective clients the easier it will be to reach them.

Product

This describes the product or service you are selling. It doesn't matter whether you offer a five-diamond service or a no frills one – what is important is that you clearly and honestly describe your product, matching it with the value it represents. Make sure your services are a) clearly defined, and b) the most valuable service in its price range.

Price

This is the amount you're intending to charge for your service. Getting the right balance can be trial-and-error – set your fee too high and your bookings will slow down. Charge too little and your diary will overflow or your customers will be wary of hidden charges or shoddy service.

"Ultimately it comes down to matching the value of your product with the price you intend to charge," says Vivi.

One price may fit all of your services, but many Celebrants have variable fees based on seasonal demand or the type of service. Do your research on what pricing strategy will work best for you.

Place

There are three aspects of *Place* a Celebrant should take into consideration.

First up, as Celebrants have to be physically present when offering services, you need to decide how far you're prepared to travel. Define the local areas you wish to service, and if you're going further afield, how much you will charge for your travel time.

Secondly, decide where your office will be, and where you will meet with clients. Kathy Speake[9] is an Adelaide-based Celebrant who likes to meet her clients over coffee at the permanent Australian Bridal Fair display. She sees this as an advantage to her clients because "… while they are there they can walk around the exhibits and check out other wedding suppliers. It's a way they can kill two birds with one stone."

And thirdly, decide which *Places* to target your advertising in. Just because you service the Gold Coast doesn't mean all your clients will come from there. Work out where they're coming from (in the *People* section of your marketing mix), and you'll know where to place your promotion.

Promotion

Promotion involves how you're going to promote yourself, and with what tools or materials. *How* could be via advertising, public relations, networking, meeting brides at expos, forming partnerships with funeral homes, or word-of-mouth. These are also called tactics.

Tools could include banners, flyers, business cards, branded pens and gifties, your website, sign-writing and so on. They can be things that you can give away to put your brand in the hands of the bride, or signage items to promote your brand and encourage recall when the time is right.

---

[9] www.kathyspeake.com.au

The Marketing Budget

A common question asked by small business owners revolves around how much money should be spent on a marketing campaign. Many small businesses and start-ups operate on a small budget; therefore, understanding how much is needed and where it will go becomes critical. Spend too much and you'll dip into funds for other business operations; spend too little, and the clients may not come.

Many times new business owners believe an ad in the paper and a Yellow Pages slot will be enough to get started. However, advertising in the phone book can be costly, and with so many people online, printed directories are not the bibles they once were. Dollars spent on an ad that may never be seen may be better spent on a stack of flyers that can be distributed at a bridal expo or for a car magnet that can be attached to the vehicle and visible at all times.

Remember, too, marketing and advertising are not the same. Marketing encompasses everything you do to get the word out, from logo design to branding, while advertising is just one segment of marketing. Prior to advertising, it is important to determine the funds needed to fulfil the rest of your marketing needs.

How Much Should You Spend?

In general, marketing experts recommend allocating anywhere from 2–10 percent of annual sales on marketing. Hard core gurus encourage their clients to spend up to 60 percent. Those that are just starting out might want to spend along the extreme of that spectrum while bigger, more established brands will spend less – the retail giant Walmart, for example, spends about 0.4 percent. These are guidelines, of course, and the amount you spend will fluctuate as you experiment with different campaigns and strategies.

Another method for establishing your marketing budget comes from Heather Martin, the Chief Operating Officer at Interfaith Family[10], a service offering resources for interfaith couples and families exploring Jewish life. Heather says her marketing budget is measured against her expenses.

"Our 2010 marketing budget is about 12 percent of our annual expenses of $750,000. This works out to approximately $90,000 for marketing," she says.

Your marketing budget will encompass any activity that gets your name out there. Advertising, design, packaging, branding, online activity, networking, exhibiting and so on. Even your business cards and with-compliments slips are included in your marketing budget.

In your first year(s) of business, I think it is reasonable to allocate up to 30 percent of your target sales in setting up your brand and promotional channels. Investing a chunk of funds initially is normal for any start-up business. So if your target sales figure is $12,000, that gives you a marketing budget of $4,000 in your first year.

The longer you remain in business, the less money you generally will need to spend for obtaining new clients. The first few years might require a higher marketing expense, but in general terms businesses can lower this expense by focusing on strategies that work.

---

[10] www.interfaithfamily.com

How to Spend It

If you're ahead of me, you've already worked out that 2–10 percent of annual sales isn't much. For example, let's say your goal is to conduct enough ceremonies to earn you total sales of $12,000. Two percent of this is only $240. Ten percent is $1,200. It's not a lot to work with!

This is why I keep reinforcing that every Celebrant must work his or her marketing dollar harder and smarter. Building a marketing plan will help you achieve this. Looking for great bargains is another way. I've included a list of the top 10 ways to promote yourself for free in Chapter 8, but like all businesses, you also need to spend money to make money.

With every dollar you spend on marketing and advertising, the one question you should be asking yourself is, "How will this dollar work to return new clients to me?" In theory, if you can't track a single booking via any particular advertising channel, your dollar is not working. My advice in this case is to cease spending that dollar in that avenue and send it somewhere else where it will work for you.

This all works beautifully when you can construct a plan that allocates enough money to attract customers but not so much it breaks the bank. This way you'll have tighter control of your spend and better idea of what's working.

The four main areas of spend will be in your branding, website creation, promotional tools and advertising. Initially your branding will chew up a fair portion of your budget, but once established you can channel that budget into other areas.

Here's a breakdown of how marketing expenditure might look in your first three years:

Activity	1st year	2nd year	3rd year
Branding, packaging	40%	0%	0%
Website	30%	10%	10%
Promotion	10%	20%	30%
Advertising	20%	70%	60%

Packaging and Branding

Unlike the creation of a product that requires packaging, a Celebrant provides a service that doesn't have to be wrapped, boxed, or shipped. The packaging is *you*! To brand *you*, therefore, hire a professional graphic designer to create a logo that represents the services you offer. The best way to determine the type of logo needed would be to understand what makes you stand apart from other Celebrants. Do you perform the services at a special, specific place? Do you offer something unique during the ceremony? What is your niche? (These questions will be explored in ensuing chapters.)

Upon determining this niche, a logo can be made portraying what it is that you do through the use of a visual medium. For example, a Celebrant specialising in destination weddings – perhaps at the beach – might hire a graphic designer to create a logo incorporating their name with the theme – such as the use of a specific bird, an ocean wave, or a sunset. Those who perform ceremonies at one specific location may use that location as a part of the graphic.

Logos can be created for as low as several hundred dollars and then used on websites, brochures, flyers, business cards, and other virtual and printed materials. Once developed, it won't need changing – consistency is the key.

Website

In 2009, Burst Media[11] found that nearly 62 percent of women use the internet to find information about products prior to making a purchase. People are conducting online searches in record numbers; therefore, in today's business climate websites are key for most companies.

Personally, I believe that even if you do no other marketing activity, at the very least, set up a beautiful, functional, professional website and you'll get bookings. We've entered an age where the internet is central to every single young person's life, both professionally and socially. Generations X and Y (and increasingly, the Baby Boomers) are going online to find what they need.

A good website doesn't have to be fancy-shmancy or super expensive. My website[12] only cost $500 to have designed and coded, and costs less than $5 a month to host[13]. For a 24/7 catalogue and sales representative, these costs are peanuts!

Thomas Witham of Day of Dreams Wedding Ceremonies in Chicago[14] read a variety of books about marketing and web design prior to having his website developed; he now shows up on page one of Google in many searches related to the search term 'Marriage Officiants'. As such, he recommends finding a programmer who knows about the use of keywords and search engine optimisation (SEO).

---

[11] www.burstmedia.com/research/research.asp

[12] www.yesidoweddings.com

[13] Visit the YesIDoMarketing.com website for recommended services

[14] www.dayofdreams.com

A good website:

- Includes appropriate search terms to rank your site high in the search results;
- Tells what you do, who you are and *where* you are (a surprising number of people don't include this information!);
- Is easy to navigate;
- Looks professional ;
- Includes contact information.

Thomas also says you should, "… get as many pictures of (you) performing weddings," as is possible. "Talk to the photographer after the ceremony and ask for copies, which will allow you to display a visual on the site so potential customers can see the type of services you perform, the mood of your weddings, and any unique traits that make you stand out from another Officiant they may be considering."

Promotional Materials

The use of promotional materials such as business cards, flyers, brochures, banners, fridge magnets, car magnets, printed pens, the website, and more can promote your business on a daily basis.

Flyers can be distributed at bridal shops for potential bride and grooms to see, while business cards can be handed out to both possible clients as well as other professionals in the business, who may in turn distribute them for you or add them to a vendor book.

Personally, apart from traditional business cards, I only have one promotional tool that I currently focus on, and that is magnetic business cards. I have one large magnet on my car that reads *Need a Celebrant? Take a Card!* I surround that magnet with six magnetised business cards – always six, so I can tell when one has been taken and thereby track results.

I ensure I arrive early at the ceremony venue to snag the best parking spot – the one where all the guests will walk past and see the invitation to take my card. After each ceremony I perform, if guests liked my work and know someone getting married, they have time to duck back to my car to take a card while I'm packing up. I generally find at least one or two cards get taken each time, and that I get a booking for every 12 or so cards that get taken. Based on each card costing 25 cents, this tactic costs me just $4 to attract each booking. Bargain!

When working out what promotional material you'll need, ask yourself what activities you'll be doing, what tools attract people's eyes, what message you want to send, and what you want people to do… all of these factors will determine where you direct your promotional items spend. There's no point in buying a banner, for example, if you're never going to have a stand at a trade show or bridal fair. Working from home, however, means you might consider a sign on your lawn.

During the start-up phase, the budget needed for these materials is somewhat higher. Once they have been created, though, you'll only need to pay additional printing costs for written material or website hosting and upgrades for the site. Therefore, the budget needed can be reduced over time. If you're really stuck for dollars, shop around for special deals. One company[15], regularly offers free business cards just so you can try their service (and they can win your loyalty).

---

[15] Visit the YesIDoMarketing.com website for free business card offers

Advertising

Advertising is not a one shot deal. The ad you place in the newspaper in January might need to be changed in April. A new booklet listing wedding services in your area might be printed in May, while the local bridal expo might be held in June. Your various ads need to be constantly monitored for relevance and effectiveness. Don't be afraid to ditch an ad if it's not working, or modify it as Kathy Speake did.

"I ask all my clients where they found out about my services," says Kathy. "Only one client in the last 12 months found me in the Yellow Pages. This year my ad will be a lot smaller."

When determining an advertising budget for the year, consider what you want to allocate throughout the 12 months but break it down to last all year. Also leave a little 'fat' in your budget to allow for those last-minute distressed-space call outs by magazines and trade papers.

Earlier we looked at how potentially your ongoing marketing budget could be less than $1,200. Considering this moderate sum, you need to be really mindful of how you're going to allocate those funds. Establish how much you dedicate to promotional items such as business cards, your website and other items. Whatever is left over is your advertising budget.

How you intend to advertise will also impact your budget. Television commercials can run upwards of $5,000 once crews and actors are paid for; newspaper ads might be as low as $50; writing advice articles and submitting them to online article libraries (such as ezinearticles.com) is free.

Attendance of conventions, fairs, festivals, and seminars may seem a costly exercise but in exchange for your time and sore feet, can provide good returns in a large list of potential clients. They also help reinforce your brand with a printed presence in the program, or flyers at your permanent display. Kathy is a huge fan of her local permanent bridal fair in Adelaide.

"I have a profile picture and brochures displayed there for a cost of $1,100 per year," she says. "This by far has been my most effective marketing technique. I get around six enquiries every fortnight and at least two of those turn into a booking."

Cheap and Free Advertising

Yes, advertising can be expensive and not always predictable with success rates. On the upside, however, free or cheap advertising can be achieved a few different ways:

1. **Contra**. Offer to write impartial articles for a magazine in return for advertising space. Generally, quality magazines pay upwards of 50 cents a word, so a 500-word article will buy you, in theory, advertising space to the value of $250. This is usually enough for a small display ad or at least a classified listing.

2. **Distress-space**. As magazines get closer to their deadline, they're sometimes left with unsold space. They'll send out an invitation to their advertisers to take advantage of distress rates – regular ad space at a drastically reduced prices. Contact your magazines of interest to be added to their alert list, or follow them on Twitter.

3. **Exchange**. If you have a newsletter or Facebook page, hook up with other Celebrants and exchange links and profiles. There is power in numbers, so don't be afraid that promoting another Celebrant will deny you a client. When

you're busy and can't take a booking, having a Celebrant in your circle who you can refer your excess clients to, in turn builds automatic return referrals back to you when the other Celebrant can't take bookings.

4. **Publicity**. If you have something truly unique about *you* – (not your client; you are obliged to respect their privacy, remember) – consider raising your profile in the press. Perhaps you're conducting mile-high weddings, or you hold the record for most number of baby-naming ceremonies in one day... if the media think you're unique they'll want your story. If you don't have a clue about how to pitch to the newspaper, magazines, radio and television stations, enlist the help of a publicist to do the slog for you. A good publicist is well worth the investment.

5. **Editorial**. If you have something of value to offer readers, submit the details to the editor and request that they write an editorial or review. Some magazines ask for payment for editorial, in which case it becomes *advertorial*. While you have no control over editorial, generally you have 100 percent control over advertorial, in turn giving you control of your brand. The downside is, advertorial tends to be boring. If I won't read it, I don't expect my prospective clients to either. Therefore, I choose not to spend my marketing dollar this way. Judge each opportunity for yourself though – *some* offers of advertorial are gold.

Of course, marketing is more than developing a brand, building a website, developing promotional materials and devising an advertising plan. Your budget may also need allow for e-commerce costs, market research, focus testing and evaluation, networking, sponsorships, customer relations and public relations, depending on how big you want to become.

Celebrate Your Uniqueness

A crucial part of attracting a new customer is communicating the single most compelling reason why he or she should book your services. You can do this by identifying what makes you unique – the one, individual feature of you or your service that sets you apart and makes you irresistible. In marketing speak, this feature is known as your Unique Selling Proposition (USP).

No doubt you've seen the Celebrant hubs online, where the visitor is served up a smorgasbord of Celebrant head-shots and perhaps a line or two about each one. You have less than three seconds to make an impression and entice the potential client to click-through to your profile. This is where your uniqueness will play a vital role. If you are using your USP to your full advantage, yours will be the only profile the couple click through to.

Consider this scenario… You want to go out to eat but how do you choose? Well, first you could determine the type of food you want: steak, seafood, Asian, pizza. You decide on Asian Fusion, but you have a dozen restaurants to choose from. Which ones have great reviews? Three of them do. So from this point, you consider the mood of the restaurant you'd like to eat in – of the three with reviews, the first one is loud and fun, the second quiet and romantic, and the third is family friendly. You might even narrow your selection further based on dietary requirements or incentives offered by the restaurant. This style of decision-making is a process of elimination.

From this narrowing down process you eliminate companies that don't have what you are looking for and choose a restaurant whose unique features match your specific desires.

Visually, the decision-making process as it narrows down might look like this:

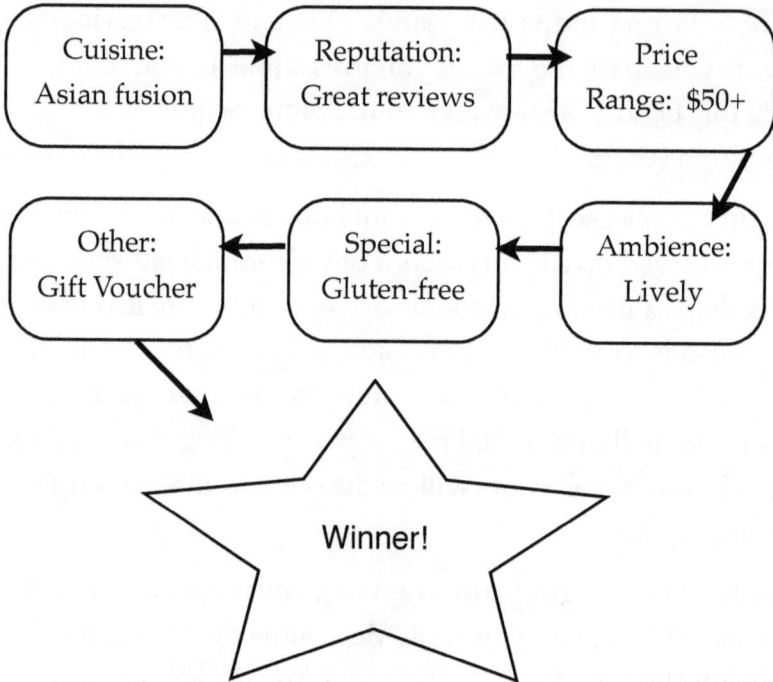

```
┌──────────────┐     ┌──────────────┐     ┌──────────────┐
│  Cuisine:    │ ──► │ Reputation:  │ ──► │    Price     │
│ Asian fusion │     │Great reviews │     │ Range: $50+  │
└──────────────┘     └──────────────┘     └──────────────┘
                                                  │
                                                  ▼
┌──────────────┐     ┌──────────────┐     ┌──────────────┐
│   Other:     │ ◄── │  Special:    │ ◄── │  Ambience:   │
│ Gift Voucher │     │ Gluten-free  │     │    Lively    │
└──────────────┘     └──────────────┘     └──────────────┘
        │
        ▼
      ★ Winner! ★
```

A couple preparing to marry will do the same. Prior to choosing professionals to work with, the couple's decision on who they hire is whittled down based on the:

- Type of wedding they want (elopement, pagan, outdoor, themed, outrageous etcetera);

- Mood they want to set for the wedding (romantic, fun, elegant, theme-based);

- Cost they can afford (or are willing to pay!);

- Celebrants that cater to this type of wedding (emcee-style, softly spoken, pretty for the photos, male or female, older, younger, priestly in appearance, etcetera);

- Specialised equipment the professional can provide (amplifiers, interpreters, poetry and so on);

- Value-adds the professional offers (gifts or discounts).

By the time the couple goes through all their preferences, you want to be the only Celebrant left at the end of the decision-making chain. You want to be standing alone. The only obvious choice. You can achieve this position by establishing your uniqueness. Showcase it, work it, win it.

By first understanding the niche population you hope to attract, you can then develop a brand that revolves around that specific niche. Standing apart from others is much easier when you have a specific goal in mind. Just as a steak restaurant wouldn't target a vegan client, you as a Celebrant should fully understand and establish what you're serving in order to target and attract the right client.

If you specialise in pagan ceremonies, *say so*. If you have an aeroplane and conduct mile-high services, *say so*. If you can sail a boat and conduct a ceremony at the same time, *say so*.

Voodoo Doughnut in Portland, Oregon, specialise in quirky weddings in front of their "… very own Holy Doughnut, under the Cruller Chandelier of Life."[16] When I visited the store in 2007, owners Kenneth 'Cat Daddy' Pogson and Tres Shannon were advertising and conducting weddings in their bathroom for $25.

---

[16] www.voodoodoughnut.com/weddings.php

This was their single, totally unique selling proposition and it was attracting world-wide attention.

When demand outgrew the bathroom, they created more room in the shopfront so up to six people can now cram in for a $300 wedding and doughnuts for six people. This unique concept has proven so popular they've now opened a second shopfront with a 700 square foot chapel where up to 60 people can share in the doughnuts personalised with the bride and groom's names.

This a perfect example of how a small business developed a USP, promoted the heck out of it, and grew big enough for a second, larger shopfront where they can now charge $4500 for "the Whole Shebang".

David Read is a Celebrant who conducts ceremonies in some of Melbourne's most unique venues and locations, including The Butterfly Club[17], which The Age newspaper judged to be the "quirkiest venue in Australia."

The club is housed in an old Victorian shop and dwelling, and is described as a "… doll-house sized Windsor Castle of camp kitsch." In a similar vein to Voodoo Doughnut, David offers beautiful weddings in this venue amongst others.

"Couples can get married on the stage in the cabaret showroom, or in any of the lounge rooms, the bars, the courtyard, the kitchen or yes, even the bathroom," he says.

"They may opt to have themed and costumed artists mingling with their guests, as well as Tarot readers, magicians, impersonators, pianists, vocalists and whatever else the couple can imagine."

---

[17] www.facebook.com/thebutterflyclub.melbourne

It's early days for David, but the important thing is, he has established his USP and is promoting it. He came up with his USP with the following rationale:

- I have extensive knowledge of the entertainment industry;
- I have access to quirky, popular venues;
- I work exceptionally well with creative, adventurous people.

Bundling these skills into one USP, David now attracts couples looking for a unique venue and ceremony that will evoke fond memories for years to come.

Being 'unique' doesn't have to mean 'quirky', mind you. Jill Z. McBride, President of JZMcBride and Associates[18], a public relations and marketing services agency in Cincinnati, Ohio, offers a creative twist to well-known marketing strategies: Embrace a cause.

"It's more than just a feel-good strategy; it's now a business necessity. The Cone Cause Evolution Survey noted that 83 percent of Americans say companies should support causes, and 87 percent are likely to switch from one company to another (price and quality being equal) if a brand is associated with a worthy cause," writes Jill in her article entitled *Why Wedding Industry Vendors Should Say 'I Do' to a Public Relations Strategy.*

To align yourself with a cause, choose a company that could matter to the majority of your target audience and that aligns with your personality as well as your company values.

Then, promote your involvement and integrate cause efforts throughout all your marketing activities.

---

[18] www.jzmcbride.com/blog

What is my Niche?

Outback Steakhouse serves steaks; Walmart is the low price leader; McDonald's dishes up fast food hamburgers.

Each of these companies has a clearly defined niche, or a specific population to whom they are targeting their products and services, and they are *known* for their niche.

The companies have purposely developed brands to attract customers in this niche by using specific marketing tactics and methods. Outback Steakhouse doesn't try to attract vegetarians – everything they do is geared towards the meat-lover. Traditionally, McDonald's is a fast food restaurant with low prices – they strive to attract the busy parents who want to 'treat' their kids, or at least feed them cheaply. Walmart offers a variety of products, from house wares to food, and do so with the proposition that you will find it there at the lowest cost possible. People who shop at Walmart do so to save money – that's what Walmart promises them, after all.

These are all examples of businesses attracting clients by sticking with, and promoting the heck out of, their USP.

As you build your own enterprise, consider what you want to become known for. Ask:

- What am I really good at?

- How can incorporate that skill into a ceremony package that no-one else is doing?

- What kind of clients will I enjoy working with?

- What feature can I offer that will persuade a bride to *pick up the phone and book me*?

Understanding the type of client you wish to attract will also help you to develop a niche. For example,

- I'm a really good 'people person' – I can handle any bridezilla;
- I only want to do one ceremony per weekend, so I need a client who can pay me for my exclusivity;
- I want to do 10 events a week, so I need clients who want a quick, one-size-fits-all budget ceremony.

Homework: Brainstorm Your Niche

Similar to the decision-making trail couples use to decide on a restaurant, use the *What's My Niche?* worksheet in Chapter 13 to narrow down your niche.

Highlight the niche you wish to occupy in each of the categories. Once you've woven a trail though the options, sum them up in one sentence to create your USP. I've provided some blank options too so you can insert your own and make it truly unique.

For example, using this technique, David's USP ended up being, "I conduct beautiful weddings in Australia's quirkiest venues that you will remember for years to come."

Brian:	You're ALL individuals!
The Crowd:	Yes! We're all individuals!
Man in crowd:	I'm not...

~ Monty Python's *Life of Brian* (1979)

Brand It and They Will Come

Some marketeers say the purpose of a brand is to foster
emotional connections with the customer. Others, such as the
American Marketing Association say a brand is to differentiate
you from the competition, defining a brand as a … *name, term,
sign, symbol or design, or a combination of them intended to identify
the goods and services of one seller or group of sellers and to
differentiate them from those of other sellers.*

A brand is all of this and more. A good brand is the complete
experience in the heart and mind of the consumer of what it is
you deliver. Deliver a beautiful experience to your client and
he or she will always connect with your brand with fondness,
in turn fostering their loyalty. Furthermore, they will find it
easy to recall your brand and recommend you to others,
effectively becoming your cheapest and most effective form of
advertising: word of mouth.

Deliver a bad experience, however, and you will experience
what I call 'brand damage'. No matter how much you
advertise, how extensively you spread your business cards,
how hard you push for bookings at trade shows, your
reputation – your *brand* – will be damaged from the bad
reports spread by your unhappy customer.

A brand is more than just a logo or a slogan. A good brand
delivers your company's message clearly. It establishes your
credibility. It creates an emotional connection with your
customer. It fosters recognition and recall. It is your promise
to the customer. It communicates your values. It makes the
customer feel good about you. And, it motivates the customer
to be loyal. In short, it's the *complete experience of what you offer.*

The important elements include:

- **Name**. Your business name should be easy to remember and roll off the tongue. It should represent your personality, your speciality, and describe what you do.

  Some people think it's important to have a business name starting with 'A' to appear at the top of the phone book listings. I don't entirely advocate this – when I asked my Facebook 'fans' why they chose the Celebrant they did, no-one picked the first one on the list. Answers included:

  - My lucky number is 17 so I picked the 17th name on the list;

  - I'm a pagan so I picked the Celebrant who had an element in her name.

- **Imagery**. Whatever visual element you choose to represent your business, ensure it remains consistent across all your marketing collateral. It should also tell a story – after all, a picture is worth a thousand words!

  To boost the 'personality' of your brand, aim to use photographs taken at ceremonies you have performed.

  Colours also convey a lot about your services – bold shades say you have a strong personality; soft hues say you're gentle and (probably) emotionally intelligent; while black and white tones say you're pragmatic and clear – there are no grey areas.

- **Descriptive**. Ideally your brand will describe what you do. A business name like *Smith Services* doesn't tell the customer what it is you actually do. A name like *Awesome Ceremonies*, on the other hand, plants the seed that you deliver… well, awesome ceremonies! To describe yourself, use the worksheet in Chapter 13, or glean ideas from some of the responses I received from my Facebook members…

- I wanted someone with a nice speaking voice;
- I chose someone who supported complete freedom in our selection of the vows;
- Feeling like the person marrying us 'got' who we were, and had an element of wisdom about them;
- Someone who was happy to do our ceremony on the moment of equinox in Central Park;
- I picked the first female I came across… Women 'feel' the specialness (is that a word?) of the day;
- I chose a female Celebrant because she was more willing to adapt the service to my needs and leave out the parts that I felt were unnecessary;
- I picked the one who emailed back straight away.

Take your highlighter and go through the above feedback again. Highlight reasons why people were motivated to book their Celebrant… words to the effect of nice speaking voice, freedom, own vows, insightful, accommodating, female, emotionally intelligent, pragmatic, efficient… Can any of these descriptions become promises as part of your brand?

Even better, contact all your past clients and ask them why they chose you over everyone else. As a common theme emerges in their answers, jump on it – here is the hidden clue to your slogan success.

- **Recall Ready**. The rule of thumb is that it takes six or more instances of exposure for someone to begin to recognise and recall a marketing message. So, reinforce your brand across all marketing tactics to promote recall. My brand, for example, is based on the repetition of the words *Yes I Do*... My phone number is 0417-YES-I-DO; my website is yesidoweddings.com; on Twitter I'm YesIDoWeddings; and my YouTube video[19] contains more than 10 references to 'Yes I Do Weddings'.

Slogans are a great way to promote recall, summarise your USP and incorporate it into your brand, and make your brand stick in your customers' minds.

Slogans

Every great marketing strategy has a strong identity... a tag or a slogan that immediately brings to mind the company's brand, USP and product. The main goal of a slogan is to leave the key message of your brand in the mind of the consumer.

I once sat next to a couple at a cricket match in Perth. We got talking and soon enough I discovered they were marrying the following weekend.

"Who's your Celebrant?" I asked, out of interest.

"I don't know," said the bride, "but he has a yellow tie."

"A yellow tie?"

"Yes, he said we could always remember him because he's the Celebrant with the yellow tie."

The couple couldn't tell me the name of their Celebrant, or what he looked like, or even what kind of ceremony he specialised in... but they *did* recall that he was proud of his yellow tie. The slogan might not describe his strengths or his

---

[19] www.youtube.com/user/AnitaRevel

style, but it did succeed in that it promoted *recall* in his client with enough information for someone to google him with.

Consider the following slogans:

- Just Do It!
- Melts in your mouth, not in your hand.
- When it absolutely, positively has to be there overnight.
- Say it with flowers.
- Because I'm worth it.
- Let your fingers do the walking.

Do you recognise the company just by the slogan? If you guessed Nike, M&Ms, FedEx, Interflora, L'Oreal and the Yellow Pages, you're right. I can pretty well guarantee a visual popped into your head at the same time – the Nike tick, the M&M dancing around, and so on. If you got a visual, it's a great sign the company's branding is working.

A good slogan works because it is sticky. That is, the group of words work so well together the customer wants to keep saying them. To create a good slogan, it must be:

- Memorable;
- Positive and catchy;
- Relevant to the target audience;
- Different to your competition.

It doesn't have to be difficult… Lyn Fox, a Celebrant in Devonport, Tasmania, uses *Your day, your way* as her slogan.

"I realised that it was my duty to ensure my clients had a ceremony that was exactly how they wished it to be," she explains. Hence, *Your day, your way*.

Tactics for Getting Noticed

OK, so you have a marketing mix, brand, a slogan that conveys your USP, a call-to-action and a budget... Now it's time to put these elements to work! After setting a budget, it's time to determine the best tactics for getting your name into the hands of potential clients. Much of this will depend on:

- The size of your budget;
- The type of client you are hoping to reach;
- The location of the wedding ceremonies you can conduct, and how far you are prepared to travel;
- The budget of the clients you are aiming to attract;
- Demographics of your client – where they live, their hobbies, how much they make, where they are shopping for wedding professionals.

I've consulted with a few Civil Celebrants regarding their marketing strategies, and in all cases, the budget is very limited. Even active Celebrants invoicing $100,000 a year should budget no more than $10,000 a year towards marketing if they go by the 2–10 percent rule. It really isn't much.

As well, after overheads such as indemnity insurance, business registrations, bookkeeping, Ongoing Professional Development commitments, maintaining suitable storage and office facilities, keeping a suitable wardrobe fresh, downtime during off-season and an assortment of stationery, there's not much fat left to make a living from. So, over the page you'll find a Top 10 list for ways to promote yourself for free. (This is also provided as a check list in Chapter 13 so you can check each activity as you action it.)

10 Ways to Promote Your Services For Free

Build a Blog

A blog is like an online journal which can be kept for free using programs such as wordpress.com or blogspot.com . By posting 200-500 word articles on topics specific to your business you can attract clients searching for your services.

If you are a Celebrant located in Darwin, for example, your posts might include information about traveling and navigating the Northern Territory, wedding venues in the area, bed and breakfast lodging in Darwin, creative weddings ideas, weddings on a budget, high-end weddings, and other subjects specific to the type of ceremony you perform.

Video and photographs can be included in blog posts and used as visuals. By utilising additional free plug-ins (or tools) the blog platform provides, these posts can then be indexed and picked up by search engines. When a person searches for 'cheap weddings NT' or 'celebrant Darwin' your posts that included these search terms may then appear on one of the first few pages of major search engines.

Get Link Love

The more times your web address (URL) appears on other sites, the more search engines like Google will take notice of you and push you up their rankings.

Get your link on other sites by setting up a 'Resources' or 'Links' page on your blog, then organising contra link swaps with other Celebrants, funeral homes, sites of other wedding professionals, tourism sites, bridal sites and so on.

Visit Other Blogs

Begin visiting and commenting on other people's blog posts, or joining forums and message boards related to weddings and your location. Leave your website URL at the end of each of your comments, preceding it with *http://* to activate the link.

Leaving a backlink is one of the most effective (and entirely free) ways of generating traffic to your site. Not only will search engines find you more easily, but individuals will too. Ideally they'll see your incredibly interesting comment and be curious enough to click on the link to your website or blog. The only thing this type of marketing costs you is *time*, though 10 to fifteen minutes a day is generally enough to spend to get your website URL sprinkled throughout the world wide web. Keep your comments relevant, respectful and conversational and your visitors will come.

Facebook

I know we Celebrants do business from the heart; we are emotionally intelligent and we love connecting with people face-to-face. But there is a whole other world that you must get involved in if you are to keep up with the Generations X and Y demographic.

It's the world of social media, and Facebook is the king daddy of them all – a mega social site with more than 400 million active users, 50 percent of which log on in any given day[20].

As the name suggests, social media is social. It's where people gather online to form virtual communities. People spend over 500 billion minutes per month on Facebook interacting with

---

[20] www.facebook.com/press/info.php?statistics

other, sharing their photos, following their favourite brands and inviting each other to events. In fact, the average user is connected to 60 pages, groups and events on Facebook. Don't miss out on these eyeballs on your profile. Build yourself a page, invite your friends to 'like' it, and ask them to share it.

The easiest way to start building a Page, is to go to anyone's Page to start with. (If you don't know any, you can start with one of mine: www.Facebook.com/GetMarriedInAustralia) Scroll down and at the very bottom left is a link that invites you to 'Create a Page for My Business'. Click on that and voila, a wizard will lead you through the process.

It takes five minutes to set up. That's it. Over time, get it populated with photos, video samples of your work, advice articles, sample readings and so on, and you'll enjoy watching your following grow steadily. Interact with the people who like your work; let them know you're human and that you are the perfect Celebrant for their wedding, funeral, naming ceremony, vow renewal , boat naming and so on.

Twitter

Yet another social media site with massive potential, Twitter.com (commonly referred to as Twitter), lets you update your status with just 140 characters. Your status is broadcast to all your followers who can then re-tweet it (send it to all their followers) or reply to it (creating interaction).

Because 140 characters takes only seconds to read, it's very popular with the short-attention-spanned Generation X and Y demographic (the generation that invented speed-dating, and most of whom have never known life without internet).

It takes around two minutes to set up an account, and you can begin 'micro-blogging' straight away. Use it to let your dear tweet friends know when you've added an article to your blog, or you've found an interesting resource somewhere else. You'll find the more you interact with other tweeters, the more they'll become willing to re-tweet your twits, (say that 10 times fast!), effectively spreading your brand and message to an audience you may not have otherwise connected with.

Write Articles

Whether you write an advice column for a bridal directory or magazine, or an information piece for an online article hub, writing a quality article establishes your credibility as an expert in your field. Credibility promotes trust, trust promotes business. Also promoting business is the profile-raising biography you strategically place at the end of every article with your contact details.

To get ideas for your articles, run through the most commonly asked questions by your clients. Then, answer them in article format. For example, in one month I was emailed four times from international couples asking me how to get married in Australia. Eventually the light went on and I realised it was a golden opportunity to write a unique, helpful article for countless engaged couples around the world. So, I got to work writing the article, *How to Get Married in Australia*, which I then posted on eHow.com[21], a site that specialises in answering "How do I... ?" questions from visitors.

Other places to submit articles include ezinearticles.com, goarticles.com, easyarticles.com and articlealley.com.

---

[21] www.ehow.com/how_5939828_married-australia.html

Free Directories

You've seen them before – the guides and directories listing wedding professionals, both in print and online. The print versions cost a bundle to advertise in, which is under-standable considering it costs a lot of money to print them in the first place.

Many online directories, however, will happily list your basic details for free – they'll make their money later on from upselling your listing to one that includes a photo, more description, web link and so on. Plus, the hundreds of links on their site serves to push them up the search engine rankings. So, they want your listing!

They're all different though, with different functions and terms and conditions, so just start by googling 'free directory' until you find the ones right for you.

Don't limit yourself to niche directories, either. Services such as Hotfrog.com.au and TrueLocal.com.au attract lots of traffic because their results rank highly on the search engines.

Guest Speak

There are plenty of business networks, community groups, charity groups, adult education facilities, schools, Universities and common-interest groups grateful to have a guest speaker share their knowledge of their industry.

Such events represent an excellent opportunity for you to share your expertise in your chosen field.

Naturally, you'll also be able to subtly convince hundreds of people why they should book *you* next time they need a Celebrant – surely they all know someone who is getting married, renewing vows, naming a baby, launching a boat, finding closure through a divorce party, or needing a funeral Celebrant, whether it be immediately or in a few months' time. These events belong to every facet of society after all, as do the members of your audiences.

Before you put the word out that you're a ready and willing guest speaker, you must have a professional and compelling marketing material that makes you shine. The materials (such as a flyer, or 'one-sheet') should offer an impression of authority and leadership in your specialisation or field.

If you want to focus on commitment ceremonies, for example, you could focus on trends in same-sex unions, current laws affecting same-sex couples, international trends setting new precedences, gay rights, anti-discrimination and ideas for equity. Make your content as compelling as your presentation and you'll win customers for life.

Network

Networking involves meeting people who are either potential clients or other business professionals that might be able to assist you in building clientele.

Networking can be done one-on-one, or in organised group meetings. Most cities have a variety of networking opportunities available on a regular basis, from morning coffee meetings to large monthly workshops and seminars.

An example of one-on-one networking that works comes from Jay Moore[22], a photographer from Baltimore, Maryland, who says, "I always try to get to know the venue coordinator and

---

[22] www.jaymoorephotography.com

share my business cards and images of the wedding after the event."

Through this Jay has been able to find additional business.

"I've booked several weddings that have come directly from venue coordinators who've recommended me," he adds.

As for networking in groups, in order to promote yourself effectively aim to:

- Feel comfortable speaking to others in a group setting. As a Celebrant you should be a natural, but if you can't, take a speech class or join a program like Toastmasters;

- Hand out as many business cards as possible with a promise to co-promote anyone who promotes you;

- Take every opportunity to 'teach' or 'tell' about what you do – at local seminars, college classes, workshops and other events. The more of an expert you become, the more well-known your name;

- Follow up on business cards. When you collect a card, contact the person and establish a rapport. Identify ways you can help each other build your businesses. Recommend them to potential clients and follow up when you have done so to see if they got the job;

- Understand the relationship you can build with each specific person you meet. How can you help them, and how can they help you?

- Get out as much as possible! Each connection offers one or numerous potential clients for your company.

Don't look at official 'meetings' as the only place to network. Each time you leave the house is a possibility to make a new client. Talk to people in the grocery store, at the bank, at PTA meetings and the kids' soccer games. Networking can be done anywhere, and the more you do it, the better the chances you have of making new clients.

Remember that everyone you meet may be able to help you obtain clients! An attorney, accountant, restaurant owner, mother, soccer coach, high school English teacher, clerk at the grocery store and librarian all have several things in common... One, they can each offer advice and expertise from their point of view, and two, they may each know someone (or know someone who knows someone) that is planning an event that needs a Celebrant.

Kathy Speake does exactly this, saying "My most successful marketing activity is *me!* In my personal and business life I am friendly, caring and professional, and this has resulted in many referrals from previous clients who have recommended me to their friends and family."

If you can't hand these people a business card immediately, tell them your slogan, and tell them to *pass it on*! I promise you, having a sticky slogan works! At one particular wedding where I ran out of business cards, I told a potential client to remember my slogan *Yes I Do*. Later, I passed a group of three mothers standing together, all saying by rote, "Yes I do, yes I do, yes I do," committing my business name[23] to memory. Within weeks I had bookings from all of their daughters who reported their mothers had recommended the 'Yes I do girl'. The slogan wasn't exactly accurate, but it was sticky enough to find me.

---

[23] Yes I Do Weddings

To find networking events, check:

- Newspapers, which often list events in the business section;

- Online, by doing a networking search for your area;

- With the local business community, such as the Chamber of Commerce;

- At local colleges that offer business courses;

- One or more of the 23 national associations for Celebrants listed on the Attorney General's website[24]. They all have conferences which are not only fun and educational, but a great place to network with your colleagues.

Co-Present

This idea comes from *The Wedding Professional's Guide: Make More Money*[25] by Maggie Magee. She suggests co-presenting seminars and workshop with other wedding professionals (such as a photographer, videographer, wedding planner and so on) is a brilliant way to get credibility and bookings.

Maggie writes, "Partnering with other industry entrepreneurs is a great marketing tool because the combined group effort will reach more potential attendees – your partners will be cross-promoting your business to their databases and it won't cost you a cent."

Of course you'll need to be ready to promote your co-presenters to your database also.

---

[24] www.ag.gov.au/www/agd/agd.nsf/Page/
Marriage_Formarriagecelebrants_Marriagecelebrantsassociations

[25] www.WeddingPlannersKit.com

Other Ways to Boost Your Business

Build a Virtual Presence

According to InternetWorldStats.com, 2009 figures show there are over 17 million people in Australia using the internet – that's 80.1 percent of the population!

You might be surprised to know that the internet realm doesn't just belong to the young'uns – only 20 percent of all Australian internet users are aged under 14. Statistics show that 67.2 percent of Aussie internet users are aged between 15 – 64 years[26]... the precise group preparing to get married, name their children, launch boats, and perhaps even farewell loved ones in beautiful funeral services. In fact, the median age of an internet user is 36.5 years old. Is this inside the age group you identified in your Five Ps? It should be!

With an audience of this size, combined with the fact it is a medium that requires active participation, you can't afford *not* to have a website as part of your marketing strategy.

A basic website can be constructed for as little as several hundred dollars through the use of a template or blog platform, to $1,000 or more for additional services such as e-commerce and SEO (search engine optimisation), or a uniquely designed, tailored site. As I mentioned earlier, my website only cost $500 for the design, but I shopped around for many, many weeks to find the right designer at this price.

At the other end of the scale, you can build a free version on Facebook or other free hosts, but the trade-off is that you don't

---

[26] www.internetworldstats.com/sp/au.htm

have your own domain name, and you don't have any say in the advertisements or look-and-feel of your page.

The amount of money you need to budget for a site depends on the type of site desired. Whatever your budget, ensure your designer and your plan includes SEO – key phrases most likely to be picked up by search engines.

Good optimisation ensures you'll appear on the first page of search results when someone conducts a search using terms specific to your business. This is critical because research shows that almost 90 percent of hits to websites come from the first page of Google search results. Furthermore, the first three results on Google will get 79 percent of the clicks. In fact, most searchers don't look beyond the first page of results; instead, they choose one from that page or conduct a new search.

Locate a professional company that can show completed, live examples of past sites, and ask about any guarantees when it comes to rankings. Ask for references from potential designers, too. Verify how long it took for the designer to start and complete the project, and to reference how many hits per day the site is getting.

Visit some sites of other Celebrants and wedding professionals to find what you like, as a visitor… as in, be conscious of what keeps you at a site and what compels you to click-through. Also take note of what bores you and what has you leaving the site so that you don't make the same mistakes when you build your site!

There are some obvious turn-offs and no-no rules for websites, 10 of which are listed over the page.

Top 10 Website No-No Rules

1. **No Flash**. Though pretty, search engines cannot read Flash files and, therefore, a site created entirely in the program will not be picked up when a customer does a search. Plus they are more expensive to create and require a more specialised designer to go in and make changes when changes need to be made.

2. **No Bad Design**. The quality of your design should reflect the importance of once-in-a-lifetime ceremonies and life-changing rituals. People organising these events want something memorable and beautiful. A casual design or shoddy layout will turn them off – they'll think it's a reflection of your personality and/or service quality. Also avoid flashing text, animated backgrounds, crowded buttons or any moving eye candy. It's distracting and, quite frankly, not appropriate for a classy site like yours. Do have a white background, white space, dark text, plain font (Arial, Verdana, Geneva, and Helvetica), left-aligned, appropriate case, (NO ALL-CAPITAL LETTERS BECAUSE THAT'S CONSIDERED SHOUTING), and consistent throughout.

3. **No Go Slow**. With the internet speeding up our whole lives, attention spans have also sped up. Your website needs to load quickly, and your brand / slogan / promise needs to load even quicker to grab your visitor's attention. When I say quick, I mean, within five seconds. Traffic statistics will show that bail-out rates are as high as 80 percent in the first 20 seconds of landing at your site. So don't waste their time making them click too many times – give them immediate gratification with a clear site that

loads ultra fast. If your site is slow, it could be that you hosting is inadequate, your graphics are too large (or there are too many), you have nested tables in your layout, non-functioning or too-complex scripts.

4. **No Frames**. Some designers use frames to keep a consistent header template throughout the site. The disadvantage however, is that search engines have trouble finding content on a framed site. They even ignore framed sites altogether! Ask your designer to use css code instead to make your layout look pretty.

5. **No Labyrinths**. Make sure your navigation is spot-on so your visitors can find their way around with one click. If a bride can't find what she's looking for, she won't click her back button – she'll just straight out leave! One way to make it easy is to use text links instead of image buttons – if you rely on images and they don't load, you don't have any links. Also, label your navigation menu so that it clearly describes what the visitor will find when she clicks on the link. Make every bit of information accessible within one or two clicks of entering your site. Too many clicks and your site just becomes a confusing labyrinth of pages. Go with the motto: *Don't make them think.* Or, an Aussie version of the same motto…

… Make it bleeding obvious!

6. **No Stale Content**. Listing events that happened six months ago, or offers that are past their expiry date, tells the visitor you don't pay attention to details. It also says you're someone who rests on their laurels, who doesn't work to keep their skills up-to-date and fresh. If your content is stale, your ceremonies probably are, too.

7. **No 404**. A '404' page is an 'error page' that appears when someone clicks on a dead link on your site, and is the most common reason visitors leave websites. It's OK, it happens – if you've got a hundred links on your site it can be impossible to keep track of them all, especially if you're constantly refreshing your content. There is one fantastic way you can turn a 404-page into a tool that works for you – check out www.goddess.com.au/404.shtml, and note how it draws you back into the site.

8. **No Fluff**. A bride has 100 items on her checklist. Reading miles of guff and fluff on your site will turn her off – she just wants what's important to her so she has one less task to do. Hire a professional copywriter if necessary to ensure you get compelling copy that describes *who* you are, *where* you are, *what* makes you special, *why* the bride needs you, and *how* to book your services.

9. **No Mystery Location**. The internet is also called the World Wide Web because, not surprisingly, it's *world wide*. You'll have visitors from every English-speaking country visiting your site, and no matter how lovely you look, it will mean jack if they don't know *where you are*. Your location is important because a Celebrant must be physically present to do his or her job. And, being human, a Celebrant is only physically capable of servicing a defined geographic region, so *make it bleeding obvious* which areas you service! Include it in your slogan or URL if you can, or at least put it up front and centre on your landing page.

   For example you could state: *Welcome to (Business Name) in Australia. My name is (Your Name) and I service (Region), (Town), (Tourist Attractions) and the surrounding areas.*

10. **No Talk to the Hand**. The purpose of a website is to have people to get in touch and book your services. Do not make it hard to get in touch! Many websites have their contact information hidden one-click away behind a navigation tab. Poorly designed websites offer a form as the *only* way for their visitors to get in touch. Clever websites have various contact methods embedded into the footer of their site so no matter what page the bride is on, the phone number is right in front of her. On your 'contact' page also include your email address, physical address, mailing address and your trading name.

Advertising Online

Websites are also wonderful vehicles for advertising online. Ad space can be purchased on many websites, including Facebook. Facebook ads may fall within a higher budget bracket, but ads can be tightly targeted and refined according to what people 'like', in real time. This is a revolutionary way to advertise – while Google gives results of what people are *searching for*, Facebook gives results of what people *like*.

It's a little cheaper (depending on your chosen keywords and category) to advertise via Google Adwords[27]. You can nominate how much you want to pay-per-click, which pages you will appear on according to the keywords used in a search, and even which specific sites you want to appear on.

For those on a smaller budget, spaces on smaller sites can be bought for much less. Many site owners agree to a contra ad swap – your 125 x 125 pixel button on their site in exchange for the same size button on yours.

---

[27] www.adwords.google.com.au

Placing an ad on a web site that showcases the community in which you work would be one way to attract potential clients (for example, on a site run by the city in which you live), while purchasing space on the web pages of local companies catering to your clientele (wedding store, photographers, DJs) would be another. Look for websites that attract the audience you are seeking.

Advertise: Newspaper and Print

Many small business owners begin advertising in the newspaper with hopes that the ad will catch the eye of a possible customer. Newspapers are valuable because they:

- Target people in your local community;
- Are still read more than news posted online;
- Cost less for advertising than larger print mediums, such as magazines.

However, there are disadvantages to newspaper advertising. These include:

- Ads are printed in the same colour as the stories. Without clever design they do not stand out from the print;
- Newspapers are generally read, then tossed away – most people don't return to the newspaper after they have finished reading it for the day;
- Ads will not reach those who don't read the paper – you will only reach the person who subscribes to the paper or who stops and purchases one on the day your ad runs;
- Those reading the paper may not need your services! Ask your clients what they like reading so you can establish the best place to put your ad.

Magazine advertising can be very beneficial to businesses that match reading audience's needs with the company's product or service. For instance, as a Celebrant you may perform weddings in a popular wedding destination area, such as the Gold Coast. A bridal magazine might feature an entire section or issue on location weddings specific to this area. Running an ad in that issue could result in several hundreds (or thousands) of dollars in revenue from future clients. Therefore the return might work out in your favour if enough people are interested in booking weddings at your destination spot.

If you can get some editorial support in with your package, you can scan the result and showcase it on your website to add further credentials to your services. This will add more value to your advertising investment.

If, however, you work in a small town not popular for destination weddings, an ad in a national magazine does not make sense. Since this type of advertising is costly, just one magazine ad could eat up your entire yearly advertising budget. Instead, locate a regional paper that features local companies and articles related to your area. People living in or visiting the area will be the reading audience, so your chances of obtaining new clients are much higher.

Thomas Witham took out an ad in the back of a small paper when he was first starting out, paying as little as he could for a three line sales pitch.

"I did in the personal section, when I started off 20 years ago. What I got from that was a bunch of sixty dollar weddings," he said.

"Those who are having a larger wedding in a bigger venue are not going to look in the back of something."

Yet he states that those who are starting out might find this is the best way to obtain new clients and build references. Numerous small-dollar weddings add up, and the photographs and references obtained from these smaller venues can create better opportunities for Celebrants just beginning a career.

Exhibit at Conventions and Trade Shows

One often-overlooked method for obtaining new clients is attendance at trade shows, seminars, and conventions. Fees for purchasing space as an advertiser can range greatly depending on the type of venue and its location, yet one thing always remains the same: those in attendance are at interested in obtaining information about or purchasing the service or product you're selling.

Two post-show surveys, (one at Bridal Bazaar in San Diego and the other in the Bridal Showcase in Washington D.C.) showed that 40 percent of future brides in attendance are just getting started with their wedding planning. Capturing their attention at the very beginning of the planning process enables you to make a lasting impression at the time they are making critical decisions.

When attending a convention, pack a variety of promotional materials that include your name and phone number. Along with the typical brochure, flyer, and business card, you might want to consider offering free giveaway items, such as pencils and pens, on which your contact information has been added. The more creative you get, and the more perceived value placed on your gifty, the better the chance you will remain in the potential client's mind long after the convention is over.

Word of Mouth

Out of all the methods you might use for advertising, word of mouth is by far the best – and it is absolutely free! Women are likely to pass on information about a product or service they like 83 percent of the time, so harness this power to spread the word about your services.

Heather Martin (Interfaith Family) has had great success in asking for referrals via a promotion – fill out a form to win a prize. As a result of the promotion, requests for information increased 45 percent over the first four months of 2010 as compared to the same period in 2009.

To increase the word-of-mouth about your services:

- Follow up after the wedding to get a feel for customer satisfaction. This can be done by sending a post card or, best yet, giving the client a phone call so he or she can tell you directly how they felt about your services;

- One of my mottos is, "If you don't ask, you don't get." So, *ask* this customer if he/she would recommend you to future prospective clients;

- Make it easy for the client to recommend you by sending the customer a few business cards along with a thank you note for choosing your services for their wedding needs.

Don't just stop at the actual customer, though! Network with the DJs and other wedding professionals at each event you attend. Ask them to recommend you for future weddings, and then do the same for them. Creating strong professional contacts with others in the business can greatly increase your chances for being recommended to new clients in the future.

Business Cards

Business cards can be one of the least expensive methods for getting your name out there. Don't be shy about handing them out. Give them to everyone, from people whose ceremonies you perform to the other professionals in attendance at the events.

In particular, pass on your business card to wedding coordinators, since they work with so many people who need your services. By establishing a great relationship with just a few coordinators you can almost ensure your name will reach the hands of potential clients on a regular basis.

A note about 'conflict of interest'... Marriage Celebrants may be associated with or promote other ceremonial business interests, but should not be associated with or promote non-ceremonial commercial activities. This means no two-sided business cards promoting other work you may do, particularly if it's within the wedding industry – pre-marital counselling, for example, or your skills as an emcee or wedding singer for receptions.

Press Releases

Got something newsworthy to share? Something that will raise your profile as a Celebrant? Write a press release and send it to your relevant media centres. Tailor the tone and manner of your release to suit each media type. Don't mass broadcast your release or you'll alienate journalists looking for exclusives. If you're unsure, especially when it comes to protecting your clients' privacy, hire a publicist.

Getting the Most Out of Your Advertising and Promotional Spend

Whatever strategies you employ for marketing yourself, the one singular objective of a Celebrant's marketing efforts should revolve around *lead generation* (which I'll explain in a moment). In short, if the activity isn't going to make the phone ring, don't do it. It's as simple (and as difficult!) as that.

Beyond gut instinct, how do you know if a tactic will work? There are some great tools marketeers use to work this out using logic and objectivity, which we'll look at now…

Media Profiler

Use the following list of questions to gather information about each advertising channel. Another version is included in the worksheets chapter to give you more room for working notes.

Make several copies, fill out one for each advertising contact you make, and then compare the answers. The trends will give you invaluable insights to the effectiveness of each channel, and will help you make decisions about which one is right for you.

How many people view the site/publication? _____

What is the cost of the ad? _____

How long will the ad run for? _____

What is the annual cost of the ad? _____

What is my CPL*, and is it achievable? _____

What is the CPM**? _____

What is the size of the ad? _____

Is there editorial support? _____

Who supplies the ad artwork? _____

How will I track leads from this ad? _____

How many other Celebrants are advertising too? _____

For online ads, how many *unique* visitors visit the page in which your ad will run? _____

How long do they stay on the page? _____

What is the click-through rate from that page? _____

Where does the company get hit stats? _____

What is the demographic of the average reader? Include:

    Age _____

    Gender _____

    Hobbies _____

    Income _____

    Education level _____

Are they qualified leads?*** _____

Additional relevant information _____

_____

_____

_____

_____

_____

* Know Your Cost Per Lead (CPL)

A 'lead' is marketing jargon to describe a person who is a potential customer. Three things happen to leads: first we attract them (called 'lead generation'); then we qualify them (rank them according to how probable it is they'll make a purchase); and then we convince them to actually buy, (this is called 'lead conversion').

Once we've generated leads, we can qualify them many different ways. For this case study, let's call our leads:

- **Hot**. Also called a 'qualified' lead, this customer matches the 5th P profile in your Marketing Mix: *People*. If they book your services, a 'conversion' has occurred;

- **Warm**. The lead is shopping around, or it's a wedding planner or a parent asking on behalf of the couple. They are ready to book, but need more time or education;

- **Cool**. The lead is unlikely to book, or has a long lead-time until he or she needs a Celebrant; and

- **Cold**. There's no chance of a booking from this lead.

Knowing your Cost Per Lead (CPL) is invaluable with helping you set your advertising budget. Put simply, the CPL is how much it costs you for every lead your ad brings you. If you pay $500 for an ad, for example, and your phone rings only once, that lead cost you $500. You'll barely cover that investment with one ceremony. If your phone rings 10 times, the leads cost you $50 each. If it rings 100 times, the leads cost you $5 each. Obviously, the lower the CPL figure, the better.

To calculate your CPL, the first step is to qualify what a lead is to *you*. Is it having the phone ring, or is it having someone book your services? In the case of Celebrancy, where each lead is usually a one-off client, I define my leads as someone who pays me a non-refundable booking fee for my services. (I'll use this definition for the sake of this case study.)

Secondly, work out how many leads you want in order to be able to make your living. For this case study, let's say you'd like 100 ceremonies a year to achieve your desired earnings...

If your advertising budget is $1000, to get 100 ceremonies a year your advertising must attract 100 leads for only $10 per lead. Your CPL benchmark, therefore, is $10. That's how much you should be willing (and able) to spend on having a non-refundable booking fee land into your account.

Remember earlier I mentioned that I get a booking for every 12 or so magnetic business cards that get taken from my car? Based on each card costing 25 cents, one booking for every 12 cards means my CPL is $4. That's fantastic! Sadly, I can't rely solely on this channel for all my bookings. It takes a couple of weeks for 12 cards to get taken – one booking every two weeks would only bring me 26 weddings, *not* the 100 I've set as the goal for this case study.

Making Decisions Based on Your CPL

So while one channel can work well for you, it may not be enough. So, the next step is to look at other advertising opportunities...

You might pay 50 cents per click for an ad on Facebook, but, per the example, if your CPL benchmark is $10, you'd need to get a booking for every 20 click-throughs. Is that achievable? Probably, if your landing page was compelling enough to elicit a response from the visitor.

You'll know if your landing page is good enough by monitoring the advertising campaign very, very closely. If you get 100 click-throughs at a cost of $50 with zero bookings, you can confidently surmise the campaign is not working.

But why isn't it working? We're told the leads on Facebook are quality leads, so the next step is to assume it's one (or more) of three factors which you must test, test and test again until you reduce your CPL to your benchmark $10.

Three Things You Can (and Should) Refine to Reduce Your CPL

- **Creative**. Is your ad headline eye-catching? Is the ad copy informative? Is the copy too vague, creating click-throughs to solve the mystery rather than book your services? Is the imagery appropriate to the rouse the target audience's interest? Once they click-through does the information on your landing page match the promise in the ad? Does your landing page have the same look-and-feel as the ad?

- **Call-to-Action**. Is your call-to-action crystal clear? Is it prominent on the landing page? Is it enticing? Is it relevant to your target audience? It is easy to claim the reward for clicking through? Is it spelled out for her when she gets to your landing page? Is the ad deep-linked to the landing page or does the visitor have to trawl through your site to find it?

- **The Target Audience**. Have you honed your target tightly enough? Are you advertising in the right geographic region? Are you targets single or engaged? Are you targeting brides-to-be? Are you speaking her language, both literally and generationally?

** Know Your CPM

In order get a better understanding of the real cost of advertising a CPM figure will help you compare each ad opportunity on an even basis. In other words, it will help you decide whether $400 for an ad is good value or not.

Since each media will have a different number of viewers (for instance, a magazine might have 40,000 subscribers while a site may have 100,000 visitors), advertisers use a formula called Cost Per Mille (thousand) or CPM.

The CPM shows the amount it will cost to reach 1,000 people. You can ask the company with whom you are considering advertising what their CPM is, or you can use the following formula to calculate the cost. You can also search for CPM calculators online to do this for you. The formula is as follows:

CPM = Cost of the ad / (# of impressions or views / 1,000)

Example 1: You purchase online advertising space for $100 and with that you are given 30,000 impressions (or views). Your cost is $3.33 CPM.

Example 2: You spend $200 on a newspaper ad that will reach 250,000 people. Your cost is $0.80 CPM.

These two examples show that the $100 ad is more expensive than the $200 ad! Of course an ad costing $0.80 CPM represents a better investment, but *only if* the audience is made up of hot, qualified leads.

Read on…

*** Know Your Demographics

Any reputable company with whom you are considering advertising will offer statistics on their demographic base. This should include the age, gender, educational and income level, hobbies, lifestyles, and location of the readers/viewers. In addition, the outlet should explain the method used for obtaining these statistics.

Online, a website might use a program such as Google Analytics to track where the visitors are coming from and what pages they are viewing. Google Analytics also includes numbers on which pages are viewed the most, how long someone stays on the page when they visit, and from what country the visitor is located when viewing.

Magazines and newspapers offer statistics on readership in media packages, which are readily available to anyone enquiring about advertising rates. Likewise, television and radio stations have dedicated sales teams more than ready to give you their demographic breakdown along with their advertising rates.

If any media channel cannot tell you *who* is reading/watching their channel and *why* they are reading/watching, walk away from their offer.

Once you have the demographics for the channel you are researching, the next step is to determine how qualified they are to be your leads. Revisit your Marketing Mix from Chapter 4 and refresh your memory: who are your *People*? If your *People* match the advertising channel's demographics, bingo, you have a potential goldmine of qualified leads.

After reviewing the demographic breakdown for each outlet and determining how hot (or qualified) the leads are, compare the results.

Let's revisit the two advertising options from the CPM section... Option 1 has a CPM of $3.33 and Option 2 is $0.80.

Sure, the Ad Option 2 might seem better value for $0.80, but how qualified are the leads? If it's a magazine for women who love being single, your leads will all be 'Cool' or 'Cold'. To get the best return, a lead need to be at least 'Warm' to be a qualified lead, and 'Hot' for you to use him or her in your CPL calculation.

If Option 1 is a website housing resources for the bride-to-be, (and this matches your Five Ps criteria), your leads will be Warm and Hot, Hot, Hot... in which case the more expensive option of $3.33 CPM is the better way to go.

Once you have allocated your budget to the best channels you can find – the lowest CPL with the best CPM to bring in the most qualified leads – the next step is to evaluate your campaigns for spend effectiveness.

Homework: Revisit Your Past

Using the worksheets in Chapter 13, do a post-analysis on any of your advertising campaigns. You might be surprised to find a campaign you *thought* did OK, is perhaps under-performing. Or vice versa; a campaign you were about to give up on is actually providing better value for return than you thought. Doing the numbers and analysing a campaign based on facts rather than guesstimates is a very worthwhile exercise.

Evaluating Your Marketing Efforts

"Practice is nine-tenths."

~ Ralph Waldo Emerson

The first rule of marketing is to test, test, and test again.
Testing is based on evaluating your campaigns regularly,
logically, and objectively, and tweaking them depending on
what you've found. Testing is so important we even do it
before we roll out a campaign, as well as during and after.
One way we measure the results of our testing is to gauge
the return on investment (ROI) for each campaign.

Return On Investment

The ROI formula is used for evaluating the financial effectiveness of your activity. It shows a bottom-line figure of how
much was earned versus how much was spent. Your ROI will
tell you what advertising methods are working and which are
not – or what you should drop for the next advertising period.

The return on investment formula (with the result expressed
as a percentage) is:

$$ROI = \frac{(\text{Gain from investment} - \text{Cost of investment})}{\text{Cost of investment}} = \%$$

If you made \$6,000 in sales from a \$200 ad, your formula
would look like this. The higher the figure, the better.

$$ROI = \frac{(6000 - 200)}{200} = 29\%$$

Step One: Track Your Budget

To evaluate your ROI, first create a marketing budget, as we addressed earlier. Keep track of what you are spending and where. If you spend $500 on a magazine ad and $150 for an online ad, write this down. (Feel free to use the spreadsheets in the Worksheets chapter of this book.)

Spreadsheet programs such as Excel (Microsoft) and Numbers (Apple) are great tools for creating and keeping budgets. Advanced users can also use the inbuilt formula functions to help evaluate your ROI with a click of your mouse.

Step Two: Track Your Leads

If you take nothing else away from this book, at least take this one piece of advice... *track your leads*. Know where your bookings are coming from. Let's say you have three print ads running, six online ads, your own website and business cards sitting on the counter of two different photographers... How do you know which of these tactics produced the lead that is sitting at the end of your phone call?

The answer couldn't be any simpler: *ask them*. It's easy. You simply say, "How did you find out about my services?"

Personally, I like to ask more than one question, but that's because I'm a marketing junkie. My clients' answers provide me with incredibly valuable information for fine-tuning my marketing spend. This way the test, test, testing pays off, giving me the best ROI for my dollar.

When I first started out, I tested two identical ads with the same directory – one in their printed catalogue and one on their website. By asking my leads where they found me, I was able to track that 100 percent of the leads came from the online version of the ad. Based on this information, I didn't renew the print advertisement and saved myself $500 on advertising that wasn't working for me, thank you very much.

Now I am testing two different looking ads with two different promises on the same site, and am in the process of tracking which one produces the most leads. One ad promises a value-add (free eBook[28] with every booking), and one promises a discount service (a one-size-fits-all service during off-season). At the time of publishing, the ad with the value-add offer is bringing me better results which suits me fine – I'm not a fan of discounting as it devalues the brand. Even so, I was obliged to test it to honour the marketeer's commitment to testing!

Testing and re-testing my ads, my offers, my calls-to-action and even my pricing, will ensure that I will end up with the leanest, meanest marketing machine I can.

Other Ways to Track Your Leads

Online statistics

Programs like Google Adwords and Analytics tell you exactly where your online clients are coming from. Heather Martin, (Interfaith Family), utilises this tool to track website usage, conversion rates, and success of her online marketing.

"We know that the key content that people access deals with 'how to do' issues and basic information – how to plan an interfaith wedding, what are the Jewish holidays about, and what is their meaning," she says.

---

[28] The eBook I give away is called the *7 Day Bootcamp for Brides*, a 7 day program for getting fit, focused and fabulous for the wedding day. It is now part of a Kit that enables you to offer this eBook also. You can get your resale license from www.WeddingPlannersKit.com

"We also know which Adwords campaigns bring the most visitors – death and mourning information, and Jewish holiday information during a holiday season."

In addition, Interfaith Family tracks the fans on their Facebook page to see how many people are accessing the company through Twitter and other social media outlets.

If you are placing an advertisement on another website, ask for a regular update of these statistics from the company. If you're not getting the promised rate of click-throughs, you can re-visit your ad, update your call-to-action, or ditch the campaign and try another website.

Surveys

A survey only needs to have one question in it – "How did you find me?" Over time a picture will build pointing you to the most effective media for your marketing activity. After a dozen of so answers to your survey you will begin to see which campaign is giving you your best leads (at the lowest CPL) and best value (highest ROI). The best time to ask this question is at the time of booking while the trail is still fresh in the client's mind.

A good marketeer will also conduct a follow-up survey after the ceremony. The primary purpose of this is to ask for referral business from a happy client. A secondary goal might be to find out ways you can improve your ceremonies, thereby increasing the likelihood of good word-of-mouth.

Coupons

Including a coupon or coupon code in your ad is a great way to track your campaigns. Make each coupon unique to each ad so that when the client hands you the cut-out coupon you can identify where it came from. If a cut-out or print-out coupon isn't appropriate, insert a coupon code into each ad, and of course make each code unique. Coupons double as an incentive to make clients act – they scream "Redeem me!", automatically telling the client to act.

Step Three: Review and...

You know you spent $250 on a listing on a popular online directory because you recorded it in your marketing budget. And because you asked your clients where they found you, you know that 10 of them found you via this website.
Of these 10 leads, nine were full-blown weddings, one was an intimate elopement (which didn't require a rehearsal), three purchased additional product from you, and one has booked you to officiate their first-born's naming ceremony. Financially speaking, this listing has brought you (for example) just over $7,000 in earnings. Your ROI, therefore, is $7,000 from a $250 spend, or 27 percent. That's pretty good!

Of course it's easy if you only advertise in one place. You automatically know where your leads are coming from. But if you have listings on 12 different websites, each costing you $250, and you're still only getting 10 leads... you're in trouble. Suddenly your ROI is 1.3 percent. Yikes!

Or, looking at it another way, to earn $7,000 from a $3,000 spend means almost 50 percent of your earnings is allocated to pointless advertising!

Why put $2,750 in other people's pockets when it could be in yours? And all it takes to keep it in your pocket is keeping track of your budget and your leads, doing it regularly, and making decisions based on your evaluation.

... Repeat

Finally, create a plan to evaluate your marketing efforts at least twice per year; or better yet, quarterly. For those focusing their efforts online, evaluate your efforts daily until you get the campaign within your CPL and ROI parameters.

Again, if your campaign is costing too much for the leads you're getting (or not getting), revisit the campaign. Tweak the headline, reposition the call-to-action, update the offer, change the image... Ride it until it works!

Focus Testing

Prior to spending the allocated budget to a campaign, marketeers often conduct focus testing of their marketing message. That is, they put mock-ups of their campaign before a panel made up of their target audience to gauge the potential success (or failure) of the campaign.

Yes, more testing. And deservedly so. It's better to identify flaws in a campaign *before* it's run, than to realise too late that you've done your dough in a dud campaign.

To recruit target audiences for focus testing, Celebrants can ask for help from:

- Networking groups and seminars;
- Celebrant Association members;
- Recent bride and groom clients;
- Potential clients (even if it's in return for a discount);
- Colleagues in the wedding industry (photographers, DJs, wedding coordinators, other Celebrants);
- Colleges that offer celebrancy training.

When you've gathered around half-a-dozen of your target audience, show them your promotional materials including your logo, brochures and pamphlets, business cards, copywriting, website, and current ads (if you have any).

Key things to ask the target audience to identify include:

- The emotions they feel when looking at your materials;
- Adjectives that would describe your company just by looking at the promotional materials;
- Items that would make them feel more of the emotions you want them to feel (for instance, would a different graphic or colour or tagline make a difference?)
- Clarity of the message – does the group understand your call-to-action?;
- What they like most / least;
- Is your slogan / brand sticky?
- Inconsistencies within your marketing materials;
- Strengths within these materials.

Use the information from the group to make changes or tighten your marketing materials. Understand if the target audience is confused about the message you are sending, or if they get a different 'feel' or 'vibe' than you are hoping to portray, you can be sure it will be the same for the wider audience you are paying good money to attract.

Pssst. Don't take any criticism personally – see it as the key you need to unlock the most brilliant marketing message you've ever thought of before.

Playing Fair: The Ethics of Marketing

You're not alone in thinking, "I wish there were guarantees." It would be so wonderful to know that your $500 ad campaign is definitely going to return 15 or more qualified leads. But there are no guarantees. It is up to us to test our campaigns until we get our mix right and have a queue of couples with their cheque books ready. It is our obligation as marketeers to do our homework, run our tests, evaluate our campaigns and respond accordingly. There are no short cuts. We must play fair. Laws exist to ensure we do!

Of course the most obvious ethics Celebrants are bound by are outlined in the Code of Practice for Celebrants[29]. The Code states that we must offer a high standard of service, recognise the significance of marriage, comply with the Marriage Act and other laws, as well as a range of other guidelines including respecting each couple's privacy.

This Code doesn't really affect our marketing. I mean, a slogan stating "I recognise the significance of marriage" doesn't carry the catchiest of tones, does it? But, it does affect the decisions we make in that we must be respectful at all times, and this has on on-flow impact how we frame our marketing messages.

The Code implies we are bound to honour the Privacy Act 1988, in that we are "… persons registered under Subdivision C of Division 1 of Part IV of the Marriage Act 1961," and therefore answerable to the Attorney General's department.

---

[29] www.ag.gov.au/www/agd/agd.nsf/Page/
Marriage_Becomingacelebrant_CodeofPractice

As for other laws that affect Celebrants, those of us focusing our marketing efforts online are bound by the Spam Act 2003. This Act has a huge impact on our marketing decisions and strategies, as I shall explain.

Spam

The **Spam Act 2003**[30] was set up to regulate commercial email and other types of commercial electronic messages. A commercial email, as defined by Salem Global Internet Website Marketing, is "Any email sent for commercial purpose; for instance, an advertisement to buy a product or service, an order confirmation from an online store, or a paid subscription periodical delivered by email."

Then there is *unsolicited* commercial email – email of an advertising nature sent without the permission of the recipient. Sending emails of this nature is an offence against the terms of service for all major Internet Service Providers, and is a crime in some jurisdictions.

With regards to sending commercial emails, according to the Spam Act you must abide by these three fundamental considerations:

1. Unsolicited commercial electronic messages must not be sent.

2. Commercial electronic messages must include information about the individual or organisation who authorised the sending of the message.

3. Commercial electronic messages must contain a functional unsubscribe facility.

---

[30] www.austlii.edu.au/au/legis/cth/consol_act/sa200366/

In other words, do not canvas prospective customers via a commercial email (particularly if it's unsolicited) as this is considered spam. Not only does this contravene the Act, it puts your business on many email blacklists and trashes all the hard work you put into building your brand.

The best practice for anyone interested in virtual (electronic) business is to move to Permission Email Marketing. This means that you ask your customers to actively opt-in to receive emails from you. You can do this via a subscription service on your website[31], or clearly state your intention on surveys and competitions you conduct at bridal expos.

> *Thank you for providing your contact details. By entering this competition you give (Your Name) permission to contact you with regards to your wedding preparation.*

When you subsequently send emails, you must provide information about yourself (or your business), and you must have an opt-out function in your email. For example:

> *It was lovely meeting you at the Bridal Fair recently, thank you for providing your email address so that I could get in touch. Responsibility for this email is taken by <Sender's Name> (ABN 00 000 000 000), <Sender's Office Address>. To opt-out of broadcasts please reply to this email with "unsubscribe" in the subject line.*

---

[31] Visit the YesIDoMarketing.com website for recommended services

Note the words *"It was lovely meeting you at the Bridal Fair recently."* This is an additional courtesy to your clients to remind them how you collected their email addresses. It's up to you how you declare how you sourced their email, but I absolutely recommend that you do. Doing so adds credence to your brand in that you haven't stooped to buying or harvesting bulk email addresses.

While we're on the issue of harvesting...

Part 3 Section 21 of the Act states "Address-harvesting software and harvested-address lists must not be acquired," and Section 22 states "Address-harvesting software and harvested-address lists must not be used."

This means that if you have acquired and stored email addresses (from any source), you are not allowed to broadcast commercial emails to the list. If you are intending to promote yourself as a professional business person, you must have the recipient's permission. As discussed, the best way to create and manage a list is to ask recipients to opt-in to your service. This has another advantage in that, rather than being a nuisance to your recipients, you are sending your message to people who are actively interested in you.

One last piece of advice... don't buy email addresses, period. You might get a good deal (500 email addresses for $10!), but you are violating the privacy of those whose names are on the list as well as doing brand damage to yourself.

Furthermore, without permission from the recipients to send them commercial emails, you are breaching the Spam Act. (And yes, if you're one of the business owners who harvests addresses from the Attorney General's website for the purpose of sending unsolicited email, this applies to you too!)

Privacy

The definition of personal information, as outlined in the **Privacy Act 1988**[32] is "... information or an opinion (including information or an opinion forming part of a database), whether true or not, and whether recorded in a material form or not, about an individual whose identity is apparent, or can reasonably be ascertained, from the information or opinion."

The Act was initially set up to guide government departments in appropriate procedures for managing personal information. As Celebrants are appointees of the Attorney General's department, by default we must respect this Act also. It is even outlined in our Code – we are required to respect the privacy and confidentiality of all parties involved in ceremonies, conduct all interviews in a private place, and provide secure and safe storage facilities for all documents and personal information.

When marketing and dealing with clients, it is advisable to have a privacy statement on your website, or a short blurb on the bottom of your emails. For example,

<Your Name> respects the privacy of your personal information and is committed to ensuring its proper collection, storage, use and disclosure. Your information will be not sold or made available to marketing agencies or similar parties. If you have any further questions relating to this privacy statement, please reply to this email or visit our website <Link>.

---

[32] The Privacy Act can be read in full at www.privacy.gov.au/law/act

Having a prominent privacy statement promotes trust in your brand. Potential clients know they will be safe with you – not only will their details remain private, but they'll respect you for your respect of the law.

Price Fixing

Civil Celebrants are forbidden to collude with each other to fix ceremony fees in their region. The importance of this was demonstrated in 2007 when, in the words of Moira Rayner[33], a freelance writer, lawyer and consultant based in Melbourne, "Dally (Messenger) agreed to settle civil litigation taken by the Australian Competition and Consumer Commission against him and his one-shareholder company in the Federal Court because, at the request of a small group of Celebrants, he had signed a letter to Melbourne funeral directors asking them to raise the fixed fee … by $50."

Despite Senator Judith Troeth defending Mr Messenger in the Australian Parliament[34], he was ordered to pay fines and costs of $46,000 in a mediated settlement. How many weddings or funerals would you have to conduct to recoup this sort of fine? A lot!

I am an absolute fan of supporting my fellow Celebrants in their endeavours. There is power in numbers, after all. I get a buzz from being able to refer a couple to a colleague when I'm unable to do their wedding. In fact, it's to my advantage to have a close network of half-a-dozen Celebrants who I can refer my excess leads to – they return the favour when they're already booked and it's a free lead for me!

---

[33] http://dallym.customer.netspace.net.au/Pgs-ACCC/Rayner.htm

[34] http://dallym.customer.netspace.net.au/Pgs-ACCC/Troeth.htm

No matter how close we are, however, I choose not to know how much they charge – I don't want that knowledge influencing my pricing strategy in any way. Instead, I glean whether I'm charging too much or too little from such things as survey responses and my lead conversion rate.

Bait and Switch

Have you ever responded to an ad for a ridiculously cheap item only to be told it is not available, then persuaded to buy a more expensive item in its place? If so, you may have experienced a deceptive tactic known as bait and switch – the bargain price is the *bait* that lures the customer in; the product is then *switched* for a more expensive one.

A Celebrant could be accused of bait and switch if he or she were to advertise (for example) $50 weddings to lure the couples in, then add a series of additional, *compulsory* charges to bring the total price up. To avoid an accusation of dodgy marketing tactics, if you offer a $50 wedding, make sure you provide a $50 wedding!

Likewise, if you advertise a tailored ceremony for $300, make sure you deliver what you promise – it's bait and switch if you later advise your client the $300 is actually for a one-size-fits-all service and if they want tailored they'll need to pay more money.

Some online directories have a function whereby you can set up a coupon. Some Celebrants include a voucher in their thank-you cards that offers the couple $x off any ceremony in the next 12 months. No matter how you get an offer out there, always honour all discounts, coupons and specials offered. If your offer is conditional, make the terms and conditions very clear, up front. If you offer a coupon, don't make its redemption dependent on additional spend by your client. If you run a special, make sure it is accessible – don't make your clients jump through hoops to redeem their discount.

In short, don't lure customers in by promising something you can't provide. No matter how tempting it might be to get the edge and make your phone ring, being sneaky only creates agitation in your relationships with your clients (and other Celebrants!) It also causes you brand damage, which, as we know, results in no referrals and long-term lost income.

Copyright Act 1968

The Attorney General advises Celebrants that, "… original musical, artistic, literary and dramatic works, as well as sound recordings, films, broadcasts and published editions, are protected by the Copyright Act 1968 [35]."

The Copyright Act is designed to protect copyright owners from being ripped off (an explanation in its simplest form!), and provides the owners with economic rights for the publication, reproduction, public performance, communication and adaptation of their work.

Copyright law is complex, so before you choose a sound clip for your radio ad, an image for your television ad, song titles for your slogan or lyrics for your website, check the Attorney General's website for clarification, or better yet, become a member of Copyright Agency Limited (CAL)[36]. Their role is to act as liaison between creators and users of copyright material, making it easier for you to stay on the right side of the law.

---

[35] www.ag.gov.au/www/agd/agd.nsf/Page/
Copyright_IssuesandReviews_Copyrightandmarriagecelebrants

[36] www.copyright.com.au

The Three Cs

You've seen boxers trash-talking their opponents before fights and politicians talk badly about their opponents during most elections. While it is not illegal to do so (unless, of course, the comments are considered slander), in the business world it is bad practice. Potential clients don't want to see it. Avoid derogatory advertising methods and campaigns. Stick to the rule of Three Cs and you'll be golden.

Avoid the Three Cs: Condescending, Critical, Careless

Condescending behaviour belittles the listener and makes them feel inferior. Your marketing message could be considered condescending if you announce, "I make the paperwork process so simple even your groom will understand it."

Critical comments call attention to errors and flaws, whether the flaws be perceived or real. The criticism can be implied (disguised by sarcastic wording) or direct (name-calling, for example).

An example of implied criticism would be if you were to urge couples to book your services "… because I'm a man; you can't trust what a female Celebrant will wear to your wedding." This is a sweeping critical observation of all female Celebrants.

Likewise, if a female Celebrant were to advertise "Women are better than men – we don't stand in the middle of the couple and hog the limelight," she's engaging in critical commentary.

Direct critical observation can border on defamation if you're not careful. If you were to begin warning your potential couples to "… steer clear of Fumble Fingers Freddy, he dropped all the paperwork in the lake last year," be very careful that the Celebrant you're referring to doesn't find out – you may lose your house in a defamation suit!

Careless comments and throwaway lines may seem harmless but in fact, if they evoke a bad feeling in your target audience it's a strike against your brand. They might include statements or slogans like:

- I offer a refreshing alternative to the 'typical' Celebrant;

- If you want a Celebrant who's OK for a Kiwi, I can recommend this one…

- You've tried the rest, now book the best.

Careless statements that carry a derogatory tone is an instant turn-off for emotionally intelligent brides and other potential clients.

The lesson in avoiding the Three Cs is, be careful of making statements that denigrate your colleagues, clients, craft and yourself! Go with Aretha Franklin on this… R.E.S.P.E.C.T.!

Homework and Worksheets

Life is so much easier when someone has done the set-up for you. In this Chapter you will find templates and worksheets to help you not only create a marketing plan, but to maintain it and evaluate it too.

> "Teachers open the door. You enter by yourself."
>
> ~ Chinese Proverb

Bonus Marketing Plan Template

As a bonus, there is a free *Civil Celebrant's Marketing Plan* you can download from the Yes I Do Marketing website. This is the *secret* link, exclusive to readers of this book:

www.YesIDoMarketing.com/mme-marketing-plan

Worksheets For Personal Use

I encourage you to photocopy these worksheets for your personal use[37], and revisit them every three to six months to keep track of your marketing efforts.

---

[37] To find out more about copyright, licensing and personal use, visit the FAQ section at www.copyright.com.au

1. Call-To-Action

What I want my client to do:

_____

_____

_____

How I want them to do it:

_____

_____

_____

When they should do it:

_____

_____

_____

Why they should do it:

_____

_____

_____

My Call-to-Action is:

_____

_____

_____

_____

2. The 5-Minute Marketing Mix

People _____

_____

_____

_____

_____

Product _____

_____

_____

_____

_____

Price _____

_____

_____

_____

Place _____

_____

_____

_____

Promotion _____

_____

_____

_____

3. Marketing Budget

Total $$$ allocated for marketing this year: _____

Allocate to the following marketing tactics and tools (annual)

Branding

- ☐ Design _____
- ☐ Trademark _____
- ☐ Other _____

Collateral

- ☐ Letterhead _____
- ☐ With Comp slips _____
- ☐ Envelopes _____
- ☐ Presentation folders _____
- ☐ Designer certificates _____
- ☐ Stamp, stamp pad _____
- ☐ Other _____

Website

- ☐ Design _____
- ☐ Hosting _____
- ☐ Maintenance _____
- ☐ e-Commerce _____
- ☐ SEO set up _____
- ☐ SEO updates _____
- ☐ Other _____

Promotion

- ☐ Banner _____
- ☐ Business cards _____
- ☐ Branded pens _____
- ☐ Name badge _____
- ☐ Fridge magnets _____
- ☐ Thank-you cards _____
- ☐ Branded gifties _____
- ☐ Flyers _____
- ☐ Car decal _____
- ☐ Publicist _____
- ☐ Expo stand inc furniture hire _____
- ☐ Other _____

Advertising

- ☐ Advertising online #1 _____
- ☐ Advertising online #2 _____
- ☐ Advertising print #1 _____
- ☐ Advertising print #2 _____
- ☐ Other _____

Other

- ☐ Networking events _____
- ☐ Association subscriptions _____
- ☐ Other _____

4. What's My Niche?

Suggested elements	Descriptions for each element		
Type of Wedding	Elegant	Casual	
Delivery Style	Formal	Ad lib	
Reputation	Reliable	Unique	
Desired Earnings	Cheap	High End	
Special Skills, Traits	Calli-graphy	Sings	
Other	Venue	Gift voucher	

My USP is:

_____

_____

_____

5. Brand Brainstorm

What is the overall theme or feel of my services?

_____

What type of graphic might go along with this?

_____

What colours would go along with this feel?

_____

What slogan will meet the criteria to make my brand sticky?

_____

What could I do to make my promotional materials stand apart from others using this theme/brand?

_____

Who is my competition? (Check Yellow Pages, do online searches, and utilise other research methods to find other Celebrants with whom you will be in competition.)

_____

What makes their services stand apart? What do they offer that I don't?

_____

What do I offer that is different from what they offer? How can I capitalise on this even more, making my business stand out from theirs?

_____

6. Action the Top 10 Free Promotion Tactics

Here is your checklist of the Top 10 Ways to Promote Your Services For Free… I encourage you to set yourself a timeline to action at least five of the tactics.

Either number this list from one to 10 in order of importance, or tick each one off as you complete the task. I don't care how you use this list, I only care that you do!

☐   Build a Blog

☐   Get Link Love

☐   Visit Other Blogs

☐   Facebook

☐   Twitter

☐   Write Articles

☐   Free Directories

☐   Guest Speak

☐   Network

☐   Co-Present

7. Media Profiler

How many people view the site/publication? _____

What is the cost of the ad? _____

How long will the ad run for? _____

What is the annual cost of the ad? _____

What is my CPL*, and is it achievable? _____

What is the CPM**? _____

What is the size of the ad? _____

Is there editorial support? _____

Who supplies the ad artwork? _____

How will I track leads from this ad? _____

For online ads, how many *unique* visitors visit the page in which your ad will run? _____

How long do they stay on the page? _____

What is the click-through rate from that page? _____

Where does the company get hit stats? _____

What is the demographic of the average reader? Include:

 Age _____

 Gender _____

 Hobbies _____

 Income _____

 Education level _____

Are they qualified leads?*** _____

Additional relevant information _____

8. Ad Tracker: Cost Per Lead

CPL = (Cost of investment / **Qualified** leads) = $

Tactic	Cost	Leads	CPL

9. Return On Investment Calculator

$$ROI = \frac{(\text{Gain from investment} - \text{Cost of investment})}{\text{Cost of investment}} = \%$$

Tactic	Cost	Revenue	ROI

10. Marketing Mind Map

Mind mapping involves creating a visual tool to 'spill' all your ideas onto paper. Mind maps are often used to clarify and organise thoughts. The process is a creative one, and the approach allows the developer of the map to see many aspects related to one specific problem. The resolution of the problem arises from considering all parts of the map and narrowing them down until a solution is found.

To create a mind map you will need:

- A plain sheet of paper (the larger the better)
- A pen, or a series of coloured pens and textas so each thought or stream can be written in its own colour.

Directions for Creating a Mind Map

1. Draw a circle in the middle of the paper. In this circle, write the problem you wish to solve. Some ideas include 'places to advertise', 'ideas for creating a brand', or 'budgeting for marketing.'

2. From this circle create lines, bubbles, short words, or longer phrases that relate to this problem. For instance, if your problem is finding a place to advertise, your concerns, and the phrases you might write around the middle circle, may be 'cost', 'timeline', 'number of views', and 'what are local news media sources?'

3. Beside each of these potential problems you are facing you can also list possible solutions or answers. For instance, next to 'what are local news media sources' you might create a list of magazines and newspapers in the area in which you officiate weddings.

4. After creating the mind map, you can then take each individual problem and create a list of potential solutions on a separate sheet of paper. If your main concern was where to find local news media sources, this would be listed at the top of the separate sheet of paper. Then, beneath it, create a numbered list of all the local news media sources you can find.

    Take this a step further by including the additional problems you faced when creating the original mind map. Next to each media source, write down the cost for advertising, the time frame in which the ad will run, and the number of subscribers/readers/viewers this particular media source has.

The problems facing your business might be ongoing (how much money is needed for advertising, where to advertise) or they might be short-term (finding a rental location, creating a logo and initial branding materials.) If the issue is long-term, keep the original mind map for future reference.

Mind maps can be used over again, and they can be added to if certain situations change (new media outlets are found, a budget increases/decreases).

Get the Next Edition Free

The contributors to this edition of *Marketing Made Easy For Celebrants* have all offered valuable insights into the way they build their business through marketing. In so doing, not only have they have raised their profile as a professional in the wedding industry, but they've strengthened celebrancy's place in the world. Thanks to them, individuals and families will enjoy more and more choice for observing life's most important and memorable moments.

If you share a vision of making celebrancy a viable career choice, whether it be for the registered Marriage Celebrant or for the ceremony aficionado specialising in life's special moments, and have a marketing idea you're willing to share, please get in touch.

Perhaps you've completed your worksheets and would like to offer your experiences as a case study. Or you tried something completely new and unique and you're happy to share your results. No matter how big or small your contribution, if it gets included in the next edition of this book, I'll send you a free copy of every edition for life.

Simply fill in the form on page 111, or email the publisher with your contribution, via www.NowAgePublishing.com

Thank you in advance!

Yes, I want to be involved in the next edition!

If you have a case study to share, and you'd like to be included in the next edition, please complete this form:

Snail mail	Now Age Publishing PO Box 555, Cowaramup 6284 Western Australia
Email	nowagepublishing@gmail.com Subject: Marketing For Celebrants No attachments larger than 2mb please

Name   _____

(as you would like it to appear in the book)

Address   _____

_____

_____

_____

(where you would like your free book sent)

Enclosed / Attached (please tick each item you're sending)

☐ A case study in full, from how you discovered or thought of the marketing opportunity, through the planning process, and an analysis of the results.

☐ An idea for the next edition – something you haven't tried yet but would like to explore.

☐ A request for anything you'd like to see included in the next edition.

Feedback

(We welcome all constructive criticism and feedback)

Permissions

☐ Permission is given to Now Age Publishing Pty Ltd to publish my contribution with due credit and my approval of the final text.

☐ Permission is given to publish my feedback for the purpose of testimonial. Permission is also granted to edit my testimonial for consistency.

Credit

The credit for my contribution should be given as follows:

(eg, your name, your business name, a link to your blog or website)

Signed

(Sign this to confirm your contribution is original and you have the right to send it)

Date

About the Author

As described on Anita's personal website[38], Anita is a creatrix, author, mother and wife, web diva, dream weaver, lover of life...

She's also a Civil Marriage Celebrant, teacher, artist, traveller and joy junkie but couldn't make these rhyme.

Prior to moving to Western Australia in 2001, Anita was a director in a Sydney-based marketing agency. Her clients included Toyota Motor Corporation Australia, the Health Insurance Commission and various smaller accounts.

Anita has written more than a dozen books and e-Courses on women's well-being, and hundreds of articles found sprinkled across the internet. She loves presenting her work to groups all around the world, as well as in virtual circles online.

Anita's heart now belongs to a farm in the stunning Margaret River region where she lives with her husband, two children and a golden retriever who is as loyal as his nearest cuddle.

---

[38] www.AnitaRevel.com

eBooks by Now Age Publishing

7 Day Bootcamp for Brides

*Feel Fit, Focused and Fabulous
on Your Wedding Day*

In all the chaos leading up to a wedding, it's easy for a bride to forget about her health. Soon she has blotchy skin, black bags and fingernails bitten to the quick. Bad habits emerge as she resorts to carrot sticks, coffee and champagne. Stress levels rise, tempers shorten and high hopes plummet.

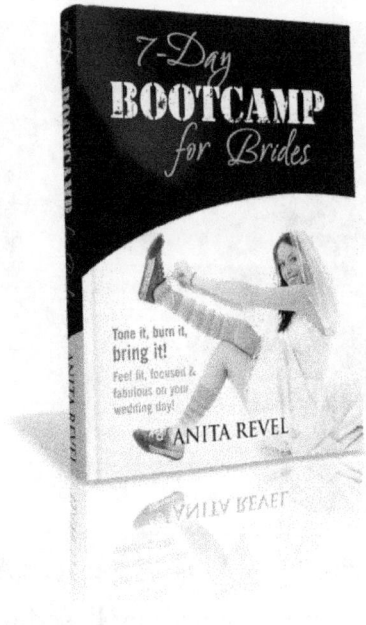

Don't let this be you! Help is here!

This guide by Anita Revel will help you regain your awesomeness in just seven days. Simply follow the tips to go from stress hag to glowing bride. Stick with the rules and you'll keep your gorgeous glow for the rest of your life!

The ideas and exercises outlined in this program have been developed by professional nutritionists, fitness coaches and motivational experts, so you can be sure it's the most practical and safe program for you as the bride-to-be.

nowage
publishing.com

The Wedding Professional's Guide: Make More Money For No Extra Effort

There are 115,000 weddings every day around the world. What are you doing to get a bigger slice of that pie?

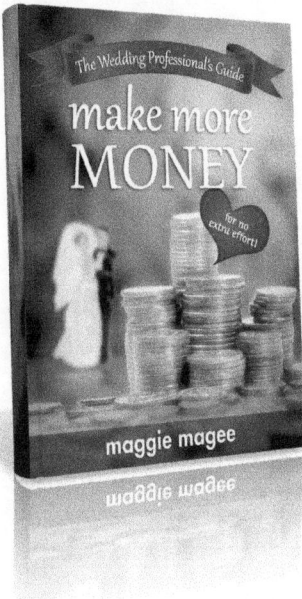

No matter how successful you are in the wedding industry, there is an easier way to make more money off the back of what you're already doing.

Maggie Magee explodes the myth that wedding industry professionals must work super hard to make it to the top – all you need are these simple tools and techniques designed to turn your business into a cash flow machine.

With this set-and-forget system you can generate a 6-figure income over your business lifetime.

What will you find inside this eBook and kit?

- What they didn't teach you in business school – the secret to getting the edge.

- How to overcome a down economy.

- The ultimate character trait you need to succeed.

- Out-of-the-box ideas to sell your services to people who normally would not hire a wedding professional.

- And so much more! Visit **WeddingPlannersKit.com** *today*!

www.ingramcontent.com/pod-product-compliance
Lightning Source LLC
Chambersburg PA
CBHW031813190326
41518CB00006B/316